FIRST PERSON, SINGULAR
A Handbook for Survivors
by
Lucy Miele

***

Cover and Illustrations
by
Paul Chase

***

Published by
Hill House
Stockton, Illinois 61085

D1114236

ACKNOWLEDGMENTS

I am so grateful to the people who have helped bring you this book. Thank you,

Frannie Thomas of Woodbine, Illinois—for insisting that the columns written "the year after" would be helpful for more people than my newspaper readers:

Melody Heidenreich of Stockton, Patricia Sughroe of Elmhurst, and John Gile of Rockford, Illinois—for years of friendship and months of loving encouragement:

Eileen Buchanan, Vice President of Shimer College, Waukegan, Illinois—for patient perfectionism, burnishing and stroking:

Nancy Schuldt of Stockton, Illinois—for special insights and perceptions:

Irma Zueger of Stockton, Illinois—for always being there:

Laurrel Vanderheyden of Stockton, Illinois—for continuing wisdom, advice, phone calls and prayer:

Margaret Laurel Miele and Vera Ruth Miele of Chicago, Illinois—for bearing lovingly and patiently with a mother who tells the world about her daughters:

Margaret Lorraine Miele of Mount Carroll, Illinois—for putting the lie to mother-in-law jokes:

John C. Frohlicher of Northport, Michigan—for helping his daughter carry a burdened packsack over a rocky portage:

Paul Chase of Elizabeth, Illinois—for insightful, creative and sensitive illuminations of the text:

Patricia B. Johnson of Villa Park, California—for singing my heart in *Lucy's Song*.

***

My gratitude to Edward Lucie-Smith for his gracious permission to quote from his perceptive poem, *The Lesson*:

Lee Schmidt, R.N., M.N., for kindly allowing me to reprint *Do's and Don'ts for Helping Bereaved Parents*, © 1979:

John and Elizabeth Sherrill for generously permitting me to quote from their book, written with Corrie ten Boom, *The Hiding Place*.

Grateful acknowledgment for their kindness is given to Hospital Publications, Inc., Tyndale House Publishers and the Lockman Foundation.

The survey, "Widows and Widowers" by Anthony Pietropinto, MD, is used by permission of *Medical Aspects of Human Sexuality,* Hospital Publications, Inc., Secaucus, NJ.

All references marked TLB are from *The Living Bible*, © Tyndale House Publishers, Wheaton, IL, and used by permission.

All references marked NASB are from the *New American Standard Bible*, © The Lockman Foundation 1960, 1962, 1968, 1971 1972 1973, 1975, 1977 and used by permission.

***

I greatly appreciate the timely assistance of Robert Weissmiller, attorney-at-law, Mount Carroll, IL; Edward Gearhart, computer consultant, Dixon, IL; Charlie Green, friend and photographer, Stockton, IL—and the unflaggingly enthusiastic aid given by the Stockton Township Public Library.

***

It is an awesome impossiblity to list all the people who have seen to it that, even without Louis, I am not alone. May God bless you as richly as you bless me.

LFM

Table of Contents

Illustrations

INTRODUCTION

When I first met the Mieles, they were the "new 6th grade teacher and his wife" who'd moved to our little farming community from Chicago. And they needed a sitter for their baby, Margaret. I was just 15, and soon was trudging regularly up the long stairs to their apartment to stay with baby Margaret and, the next January, baby Vera. Lucy always drove me home at the end of the evening, and we would sit in the car in front of my parents' home and have long talks into the night about school and college and literature and boys.

In the years that followed, Lucy and Louis and the girls moved to the big brick Hill House in the country, and I went off to college. When I returned to marry my high school sweetheart, our families became extended families to one another. Together, we did the things families do in the country—we had hay rides and sleigh rides, cut firewood and pressed cider, helped paint the little Morseville Church down the road, and had wonderful pot-luck suppers followed by singing by the fireplace in the Hill House library.

Lucy and I became dear, close friends. We coffee-ed together, breakfasted together, lunched together, laughed together and cried together. When I was troubled, I always knew that at Hill House there would be a light lit, a fire burning in the library hearth, a cup of tea, a soft chair, an understanding ear and loving counsel.

In that bitter January when Louis died, we all grieved for the loss of this gentle, quiet man. . .and grieved again in the days and weeks and months that followed for the ache and loss and loneliness of his family. Widowhood is so personal a grief, however, that it was the one trip that Lucy took alone. Her book is the accounting of what she met along the way.

For those of you who may right now be living such a grief, and for the rest who inevitably will, Lucy's book is the light lit, the fire burning, the understanding ear and the loving counsel that will ease your journey.

Melody Parker Heidenreich
Stockton, Illinois

For Louis . . .

PROLOGUE

It was the first of the awful winters. Continuous cold since Christmas. Constant snow. Drifts barricaded our big, old, brick farmhouse out in the hills of Jo Daviess County, Illinois. The country roads were single tracks, burrowing between mountains of snow.

We'd had a beautiful—if unusual—Christmas. It was unusual in that never had I known my husband, Louis, to be so thoughtful. We'd been married on a Christmas Eve day, nineteen years before—which is a rotten time to have an anniversary. The marking of it gets lost in the Christmas preparations.

But that afternoon, my husband went to town and came back with a huge pink azalea plant for a "happy anniversary". I was simply overwhelmed. It was the first anniversary present as such he had ever given me. I quickly went and got his "happy anniversary" present from under the tree. (It was a pair of leather work gloves.)

This thoughtfulness continued on through January. (Oh, it was always there, but there were more demonstrations of it than before.) My birthday is January 3—which is a rotten time to have a birthday. The glow of giving is reduced to the charred residue of a burned-out bank account.

But the day before my birthday my husband snapped up our bedroom shades, awakening me. "Grr, mummmble, grummmble," I protested sleepily. "This is a vacation day. We get to sleep in."

"You can sleep as late as you'd like," he said, "but I have an idea for when you do get up."

I groaned. Every time he had an idea, it involved something constructive like taking down the Christmas tree or balancing the checkbook. You know. Fun stuff.

He ignored my rampant apathy and continued. "When you do get up, let's go shopping for those slippers and gloves you want for your birthday."

Never have I awakened more fully, more joyously, more vigorously. I bounded out of bed so fast Louis was almost trampled in the rush.

We left a note for our sleep-in daughters on the refrigerator door (where they'd be sure to find it) and took off.

We had a delightful time. Louis had never gone shopping *with* me *for* me before, and it was the most elegant feeling possible to have a tall, dark, handsome man around, carrying both packages and money.

And after we'd done the shopping, he took me out to lunch. (I happen to think LunchOut is one of civilization's greatest contributions. It is followed only by BreakfastOut and DinnerOut.)

So it went throughout January.

My husband was a sixth grade teacher up in the village, and the winter of 1978-79 was so horrendous that the Stockton School District called a lot of "snow days". (If the roads are so impassable the school buses can't get through, we get a snow day.)

We loved snow days. They were "found" days. There were no plans to be worked out, no obligations to keep, nothing that needed doing. There was absolutely nothing we had to do.

Our daughters and I were planning to go to a United Methodist Prayer and Praise Retreat the last weekend in January. Louis didn't care to go, but he always encouraged us to go if we wanted to.

And here I'd like to explain a little bit about my spiritual adventure.

About five years previously, I was stumbling through a vast, barren, arid spiritual desert. I felt as if I were walking around with broken glass in my stomach. I hurt.

I wondered why people acted as if I were normal—how I could perform the usual, expected tasks of wiving and mothering, when I was lost—so lost.

And then some friends invited me to a home Bible study. I was offended. Why did they think I needed a Bible study, freavensake. But something (or Someone) made me accept. For the first three meetings I sat, silent and sulking in the corner. And the miracle happened. I truly came to know the Lord Jesus Christ. My desert blossomed. I came from plodding desolation into joyous, happy life.

I can get argued down on lots of things, spiritual and temporal, but the reality of that experience is the foundation on which the rest of my life has been built. Not only did I discover, viscerally and forever, what the love of

God is but—all of a sudden—I could smile in church.

You have no idea how this appealed to me. Previously, I'd thought of church as a duty, and a pretty boring one at that. It was a place to mentally construct my newspaper column, to write grocery lists, to think about what I'd fix for Sunday dinner.

Oh, we'd always gone to church, but I don't know who I was pleasing by it. Certainly not God.

But, suddenly, I started listening to all the things I'd heard in church for years. My faith changed my life and my home and my marriage. The last five years of that marriage were absolutely glorious. My husband and I had a wonderful time. He wasn't into the spiritual joys I was experiencing (and I frequently worried and prayed about his seeming lack of spiritual adventures) but we were more content together than we'd been through our entire married life.

All the "happy" phrases in the Bible jumped out at me—words like "joy" and "love" and "health" and "prosperity". I didn't exactly skim over all the information in the Bible about how God is our help in time of trouble—but I wasn't in big trouble, so it didn't imprint itself on me.

At any rate, our daughters and I were scheduled to go to the retreat on Friday. On Wednesday it started snowing and a snow day was called for Thursday. It was a beautiful day.

I was learning how to sew and worked in my office, just off the dining room. Louis was caning a chair, so he set it on the dining room table. We laughed and talked and showed each other our progress—he was so proud of my sewing, and proud of the fact that I'd made him a handsome brown turtleneck shirt. He wore it everywhere.

When I tired of sewing and went into the library to sit by the fire and crochet, he carried his chair in there to work on. Sometimes we just sat by the fire and drank tea together.

We spent that whole day together, with the snow falling thickly and softly around the house.

The next day, Friday, was also a snow day, so the girls and I decided not to go to the retreat that day. Instead, the whole family piled in the car and drove twenty miles to the Farm-and-Fleet store. (On a snow day, the school buses can't get through, the milk trucks can't get through, but we can get through.)

At the Farm-and-Fleet, Louis bought us a blender and also bought me a full-length mirror to hang on the closet door in the dining room, so I could see what I was doing with my sewing.

We also went to a fancy super-market to get some fruit. As is the insidious habit of super-markets, several handsome enameled tin trays were also displayed in the produce section. I wanted one.

"Lucy," Louis protested, "you don't need one more tray!"

He was right. I didn't need another tray, another basket or another crock for that matter—yet I still acquired them somehow. I had enough money in my purse, but he was so unusually obdurate that I decided not to buy it. I knew if I did, he'd be irritated at me all the way back to Stockton. The ride home was more pleasant than it might have been.

That evening I spent a lot of time on the phone, trying to line up transportation to the retreat the next day. We only had one car, and I felt that I shouldn't leave Louis alone at home without it. Finally a friend with a van volunteered her vehicle, but only if I would drive it. Our village people get a little nervous about driving in Chicago.

We were scheduled to leave very early the next morning. Louis got up with me at 5:30 and then went back to bed. Our ride came at 6:00.

The girls went out, but I (wearing my heavy winter coat and boots) stumped through the house to the bottom of the stairs. I was going to call "goodbye" up to Louis.

But instead I climbed the stairs. I leaned over the bed, snuggled my arms under his shoulders, kissed him good-bye and said, "I love you, Louis. And don't you forget it!"

He reached up, put his arms around me, kissed me and replied, "I love you, too."

Those were the last words we ever spoke.

Columnist's husband dies in doctor's office

STOCKTON — Louis Miele, 49, husband of Sunday Register-Star columnist Lucy Miele, died Saturday afternoon in a doctor's office apparently of a heart attack.

He had been a sixth-grade teacher in Stockton the past 17 years.

Arrangements were being completed by Hermann Funeral Home.

Louis R. Miele

STOCKTON — Services for Louis R. Miele, 49, a Stockton school teacher the past 17 years, who died Saturday in a doctor's office apparently of a heart attack, will be at 2 p.m. Tuesday in Wesley United Methodist Church. Burial will be in Morseville Cemetery.

Friends may call from 7 to 9 p.m. today at Hermann Funeral Home. A memorial fund has been established.

He was the husband of Lucy Miele, Sunday Register-Star columnist.

Surviving besides his wife are two daughters, Margaret and Vera, both at home, and his mother, Margaret Miele, Mount Carroll.

Page 10   Freeport (Ill.) Journal-Standard, Monday, January 30, 1978

LOUIS R. MIELE

STOCKTON — Louis R. Miele, 49, of Stockton, died at Drs. Williams and Rachuy's office Saturday afternoon of an apparent heart attack.

He was a sixth grade teacher for 17 years in Stockton schools, received his B.A. degree in sociology from Roosevelt University, did graduate work at University of Chicago and course work at Macalester College, St. Paul, Minn., and the University of Illinois. He was a constituent of Wesley United Methodist Church in Stockton, one of the founders of the Heritage League of Northwest Illinois, past president of Stockton Education Association and was currently a vice-president and chief negotiator. He was a Korean War veteran.

Born June 4, 1928, in Newark, N.J., he was the son of Mrs. Margaret (Nielen) Miele. He married Lucy M.E.H. Frohlicher, a former Journal-Standard correspondent, Dec. 24, 1958, in St. Paul, Minn.

Surviving are his widow; two daughters, Margaret and Vera, both at home; and his mother, Mrs. Margaret Miele of Mount Carroll.

Funeral service will be at 2 p.m. Tuesday at Wesley United Methodist Church, with the Rev. Howard T. Leach, pastor, and the Rev. John C. Ferguson of Chicago, officiating. Burial will be in Morseville Cemetery in rural Stockton.

Friends may call from 7 to 9 p.m. tonight at Hermann Funeral Home in Stockton.

A memorial fund has been established.

—

CHAPTER ONE
THE END

I sat, singing, in a church in a Chicago suburb. My daughters were involved with other teenagers at the side of the room, and I was sitting with one of my Stockton friends. We'd had morning worship, topic groups and lunch. People were drifting back into the sanctuary, where a bright, energetic, young couple with hand-held microphones led us in song. Retreat songs are different from Sunday songs. They are joyous and hand-clappy.

A young woman came down the aisle from the back of the church, leaned over and whispered something to my friend, who rose and followed her back up the aisle.

I wondered what was happening, but continued clapping and singing as the song leaders revved us up to praise the Lord. The same young woman returned and asked me to follow her. "What's wrong?" I asked on the way up the aisle. She didn't say anything and I walked into a handsome reception room at the back of the church. My friend was there, weeping.

"What is it?" I cried as I ran to her and put my arms around her. "Is there something wrong at home?"

"Be strong, Lucy," she whispered through her tears.

"What do you mean? Is it me?" I said.

She nodded "yes."

"What is it? What is it?" I demanded.

She continued crying, unable to speak.

I got very angry. "What is it?" I shouted. "Is it Louis?"

Still just tears. And I knew. With weary knowledge I whispered, "Please. Tell me."

"He's dead," she finally said.

"I think I'd better sit down," I said, and stumbled into a large, over-stuffed chair. But no sooner was I down than I wanted to get up. Hands pushed me back into the chair. How I resented those hands.

"Let me up," I said. "I've got to go get Margaret and Vera."

"Someone will get them," was the reply. By this time, the lounge had started to fill with people who were praying. I didn't want praying. I wanted my daughters.

They walked through the group of people toward my chair. My younger daughter, Vera, was already crying. I learned later that the news had been whispered to the song leader who, in her shock, said into the microphone, "Oh, no. That's Lucy's husband." So they knew something was wrong.

My unreasoning anger at my friend for not telling me immediately about Louis made me call to them from my chair as they approached, "Oh, girls. Daddy's dead. We'll be all right. We'll be all right."

Then I asked, "What was it?"

"A heart attack," she murmured.

All around me, people were weeping and the girls were crying. I didn't. I understand that frequently, when someone loses a loved one in death, there is a period of disbelief. I didn't have this. From the moment I guessed that Louis was dead, I knew it was so—that it was true. Not once did I disbelieve it. How often, during the long nights ahead, did I yearn for disbelief.

And then I knew I had to phone his mother, before she heard it by the grapevine. I had to phone my father and my minister and my doctor.

It was like pushing through a hostile forest to beat through the people to a tiny telephone cubicle. And there I discovered I had lost my motor coordination. My hands were so paralyzed I could hardly unsnap my wallet. Somehow I got out my credit card and dialed the first number—but after that, I couldn't function at all. A man who led the retreat had to do it for me.

And I called my mother-in-law—out in the little, old, converted schoolhouse where she lives, not seven country miles from us. And I told her that her son was dead.

Then I telephoned my minister, and he immediately drove those cold, frozen miles to her and stayed there all afternoon until we could drive back from Chicago.

Then I called our doctor, who was in tears. "We tried to get him back," he kept saying. "For a minute once, I thought we had him, but he slipped away again."

"Where is he?" I asked.

"They took him up to the funeral home. I thought that's what you'd want."

I nodded, unable to speak. What I want? What I want? My husband at the funeral home? No! All I wanted was to go home.

Finally, we assembled our coats and boots and the people who had gone into Chicago with us. As we stood in the narthex of the church, a group gathered with us, put their arms around me and the girls, and told us that they knew that Louis was with the Lord—that he had gone home to Heaven.

"I don't believe you," I said. "I wish I could, but I just don't believe you."

These were people who had bet their lives—literally—on Jesus Christ. Although they loved me, they loved Jesus more, and they wouldn't (even in time of sorrow for me) offer soft, false comfort. But I needed more than their assurance. They put their arms around us and prayed that I would get the confirmation I needed.

Dry-eyed and frozen-faced, I drove the van back from Chicago. What else could I do? I couldn't sit in the back and offer comfort to my daughters, for I had none to give.

And, during that long, bitter drive back to the hills of northwestern Illinois, a boring, banal song kept repeating itself in my mind. The Germans have a word for it—a "worm in the ear"—and that's just what it was. A song that would not leave me.

It was not a song we'd sung at the retreat. As a matter of fact, it is a chorus which I dislike, for I consider the tune empty and meaningless.

"The joy-hoy of the Lor-hor-hor-hord is my strength;
The joy-hoy of the Lor-hor-hor-hord is my strength;
The joy-hoy of the Lor-hor-hor-hord is my strength;
The joy-hoy of the Lor-hord is my strength."

My face was numb. My heart was numb. I went mechanically through the motions of driving, my soul pleading with God.

"Oh, no, Father. Can't you give me *Blessed Assurance* or *Trust and Obey?* I hate this song!"

And I consciously wrested my mind into another song. But before I knew it, I was right back into the joy-hoy of the Lor-hord.

So I finally decided that the Lord wanted me to learn something from it. At first I thought, "Lord, I guess you'll have joy if I'm strong about this." But I knew I couldn't be strong.

Then I decided that it would be the Lord's joy to give me the strength I needed to face Louis's death—and I mused on this all the way home.

We got back to our little village after dark. We delivered the riders, returned the van, and a friend put us in her car to take us home. But first we stopped at the home of the nurse who had been in the doctor's office that day.

It seems that, around noon, my husband had experienced some chest distress. He lay down on the sofa in the library, but that didn't help. So he got in the car and drove up to town to the doctor's office. He walked in smiling apologetically, saying he didn't know if he really needed a doctor but he didn't feel too well. While they called the doctor downstairs from his lunch, Louis took off his coat and boots. Then he went into the examining room and died. Just like that. They tried and tried to get him back.

The nurse told me that he went very gently, very quietly. I'd like to believe this is true. Sometimes I have doubts about all the gentle, quiet deaths. I think people try to give comfort to survivors by saying death is less rending than it actually is. But it was no comfort to me—then—when people said, "At least he didn't suffer." The method of his dying meant nothing to me. He was dead. That was the inescapable grief which nothing could mitigate.

I wanted to get the keys to our car so I could drive it home, but nobody seemed to know where they were. Finally my friend drove us down the deserted Main Street, past the doctor's office with our car sitting out in front— the only car on that snowy, dark street.

She drove us out of town and down the snow-packed highway. The headlights of the car picked out snow glints in the darkness. She turned onto the gravel road and started climbing the icy hills to our house.

The impelling force in my head, ever since I learned my husband was dead, was "home". All I'd wanted to do was *go* home. But I hadn't thought about *coming* home—about what that would mean.

As we came over the crest of the hill by our house, we saw that all the yard lights were on. Every light in the house blazed through the frozen night. There were cars lining the lane.

We didn't come home alone. Six of our closest family friends had come down to the house and had waited and prayed for us, all that bitter, long afternoon. I'll never forget it. We stumbled through black snow and into a warm house, filled with light and love. Our daughters walked into open arms.

And as I took off my coat, I saw the mirror—the mirror Louis had bought me (was it only yesterday?) to help me with my sewing. He had hung it on the closet door that morning. And gone to town. And died. The last thing my husband did, he did for me.

And that's when I cried.

***

My six friends had picked up the newspapers, taken down the ironing board, hauled the empty fruit jars out to the back room, made soup and coffee, built a fire in the fireplace and waited for us. And then people started coming.

On into the night they came. Neighbors came. Colleagues came. Friends came. My darling mother-in-law came.

She had now lost both her sons to death. There was no one left for her, but two granddaughters and me. She was desolated. I felt her desolation—and had nothing to give but my tears. I knew they weren't enough.

Finally, everyone left. My daughters and I sat by the fire and I did something stupid. I thought I was being pragmatic and honest and fact-facing. That's my only excuse for what I did to them.

"It may be that we have to leave here," I said. "I don't want to, but we may have to go

somewhere else so I can support us. And we
have to make up our minds to be willing to go,
if that's what God wants us to do. After all, we
do want to go where He has the biggest blessing for us."

Stupid. Cruel. Unnecessary. My daughters had just had the biggest foundation wall of
their lives ripped away from them—their
father. And immediately I confronted them
with the loss of yet more foundation walls—
their home, their village, their school, their
friends.

Ah, well. There is much in my life I
would recall and rework, and the first thing I
would change is my handling of my daughters'
grief. But I didn't know any better.

We cried a bit. We hugged. They went
upstairs to their bedrooms and I tucked them
in. And then I went into our bedroom.

Oh, it was cold. As cold as death. I kept
thinking, "I wish I felt as if I were in a dream,
but I don't. I know all too well what has happened. Louis is dead. He's dead! Oh my God—
what will I ever do without him? How can I live
without him!"

And then I did something I'd never done
before, but I'd heard someone say it worked. It
makes no sense at all. Even as I did it, I knew
it made no sense. But I did it.

I call it playing the God Game, and I did it because I really needed to hear from God. Unlike lots of enviable souls, I don't seem to hear God very well. I don't have angel visitants or visions or dreams or big, loud voices or still, small voices. I wish I did. I wish God dropped enormous red-and-white billboards from the sky that read GO! or STOP! or RETHINK IT, DUMMY!

But at a time when I was so lonely, so uncared for, so unloved, I had to hear from God. I had to hear that He was still in my life, still caring and still loving.

The rules for the God Game are these— when you've got overwhelming trouble (and I qualified), when you don't know where to turn, you place your Bible on its spine and hold the covers tightly together with your hands. Then you withdraw your hands suddenly and the Bible falls open. You start reading down the open page until you come to what God wants to tell you.

Now, your Bible will open in the middle, won't it? And in the middle is the book of Psalms, isn't it? And the book of Psalms has something for everybody all the time, doesn't it? So it's really a dumb game. You could just open the Bible to Psalms and start reading, couldn't you?

But I couldn't. I needed something more—some indication that I truly would not be left comfortless. "OK, God," I muttered. "I don't believe this, but I'm going to do it."

I closed my eyes and, according to the prescribed ritual, opened my Bible. And it didn't fall open in Psalms. It opened in the book of Nehemiah.

Now, Nehemiah is not one of my "big" books. I don't read it all the time (like never) so its pages are not well thumbed. Nor is my Bible accustomed to opening there. As a matter of fact, I hadn't the slightest idea where it was. (Nehemiah is between Ezra and Esther, in case you're interested.)

"Oh, God," I thought. "Nehemiah?"

But I started reading in Chapter Eight. And God is so good—He even made it easy for me to remember exactly where His message was. At the ninth verse I let out a whoop. My younger daughter ran into the bedroom crying, "What is it, Mommy? What is it?"

"Oh, honey. Listen to this. Nehemiah 8:9,10 and 11. 'Don't cry on such a day as this! For today is a sacred day before the Lord your God. It is a time to celebrate with a hearty meal, and to send presents to those in need, for *the joy of the Lord is your strength.* You must not be dejected and sad!' "(TLB)

I'd had no idea that the song—the "worm in my ear"—that had twisted in my mind all the way home from Chicago was even based on scripture. And this was my confirmation. The confirmation my friends had prayed for—was it only that afternoon? I knew that somehow, somewhere, Louis had met our Lord. I knew that Louis was with Him, and that I'd be there too, someday.

But someday was too far away. Thus began the longest night of my life. The wind wuthered around the eaves, shuddering the windows in their sashes. The oil burner kicked on downstairs, doing nothing to alleviate the chill in our bedroom. I huddled on my side of the bed, curled up into a tight ball. And, as that awful night wore down into morning, I contemplated death. Not my husband's, but mine.

I knew I had a family—two daughters who needed me. I knew that Louis's mother needed me—she had no one, now. But none of that entered into my contemplations. I needed Louis. Without him, I needed death. It was that simple. If God were, in fact, a loving and caring God, I would die that night and go home to be with Louis and the Lord. In that order.

Morning came—and death didn't. Not for me, at any rate.

I'd never felt so cheated. I truly could

not believe I was still alive. The loving, caring God I'd worshipped was a fraud—a hoax—a hater. In the twistiness of my grief, I railed at God—not because Louis was dead, but because I was still alive. My husband's death paled in significance to my own life. God failed me.

But the fact that life (however abhorrent) goes on, kept me going on. Somehow I got the girls up and we got dressed. And then, though I didn't know it was the sensible thing to do, I found clothes for Louis. White shirt, the silk tie my mother had brought him from Italy, blue suit—I even had socks, shorts and dress shoes.

And then we pushed out into that frozen morning to drive up to town to the funeral home.

My mother-in-law was already there when we walked in. All the surviving Miele women hugged each other, and then I turned to the funeral director.

I had no fund of small talk—about the snow, the cold, the weather—anything. All I wanted to discuss was the "arrangements".

"I have two daughters to support now," I said bluntly. "I need to do this as cheaply as possible."

Bless that funeral director's heart! Not once did he try to pressure me into anything but exactly what I wanted. Not once did he say, "Just let me show you what I have." His least expensive casket was in storage and he offered to haul it out to show me. But I didn't care what it looked like. I just wanted things done decently and in good order.

(My recollection of that day shames me, for I can't remember anything substantive about my daughters or my mother-in-law. I know I must have tried to comfort, tried to uphold, tried to consider them. But my own loss was so numbing, so paralyzing, so anaesthetizing, that even now—all these years later—I can only pray I helped them somehow.)

When we completed the arrangements, the funeral director gestured to the desk. On it were Louis's wristwatch and a pile of loose change.

I looked at them and said, "Where's his wedding ring?"

He was surprised. "You want his wedding ring?" he asked.

"Of course," I said firmly. "I gave it to him."

He went downstairs, took the ring from my husband's dead hand and brought it up to me.

"Thank you," I murmured, and we left.

(I still don't know if wanting Louis's

wedding ring was right or wrong or showed an excess of practicality or an excess of sentiment or if it showed anything at all. And I don't care. In that incredible acting out of life's greatest tragedy—death—I played my part and spoke my lines with no regard for audience.)

We came home and entered a smoke-filled house. A young friend of ours had come by to be of service. He started a fire in the fireplace, but didn't open the damper.

At least it gave us something to do. We opened the damper and then ran around opening doors and windows to the -10 degree cold, rebuilt the fire and finally, sat in front of it.

He so badly wanted to do something to ease our grief that I finally said, "Would you help me get Louis's clothes out of our bedroom? I just can't stand seeing his things. I don't care what you do with them—keep them, wear them, burn them, share them, but—please— just get them out of here?"

"Of course," he said, and in less than thirty minutes we had most of Louis's clothes out of the house. I couldn't bear to give up all the sweaters I'd made for him, and I couldn't give away the brown turtle-neck I'd sewn for him, and I still (after eight years) use his wedding anniversary work gloves while stacking and hauling wood. But we got most everything else out.

***

I discovered later that this is very wise. This is a "recommended course of action" in what psychologists call "grief work". But not then—or later—did we ever do anything because it was recommended, whether by books or friends or family.

For one thing, I was incapable of seeing the consequences of an action, no matter who thought it was a good idea. For another, I was still furious at God. I decided that since God had gotten us into it, it was up to Him to get us out. "Over to you, God! I can't do it, so You'd better!"

***

Then people started coming. All that Sunday afternoon, people came mile-upon-snow-bound-mile to our house. They came bearing the universal "I love you"—casseroles and cakes and potato salad. Several farmers from down in the valley drove up with end-loaders (big scoops) on their tractors. They fought that awful cold and snow and totally cleared our winding lane of snow. They scraped out our side-yard to make room for cars. They plowed for three hours that afternoon, piling snow mountains twenty-five feet high around the perimeter of our yard. And they wouldn't even come in for coffee.

The township road truck came by and spread gravel and cinders up and down the lane and in the side yard. No charge. Someone just thought it needed doing.

Three men and a small boy spent that Sunday afternoon out in a woodlot, cutting wood for us. (One was the husband of the woman who'd had to tell me of Louis's death.) They came with their pickup truck and unloaded the wood after dark. They just wanted to say "we care"—and they didn't know how to bake a cake.

Our optometrist and his wife drove out from their city home. They brought with them an extravagant offering of fresh fruit, piled high on the same enameled English tin tray I'd coveted in the supermarket. For years that tray has been a comforting reminder to me that (once) I did something right—that I didn't buy it and ruin my last, lovely day with Louis.

My father flew in from New York. My brother flew in from Washington, DC. And somehow, in all that bustle of bereavement, people took care of my daughters. People talked to them and prayed with them and comforted them. I couldn't.

The library was comfortably full of

people. All afternoon. All evening. All the next day.

I didn't know what was expected of me, so I didn't do it. Somehow the training of years took over. I have a heritage of hospitality from my parents. I had learned to open a house to people all through my formative years, and Louis and I had rejoiced in hosting friends. His favorite entertainment was having in a small group (never more than eight) for dinner and conversation. Me? I liked that, too, but I really loved big bashes, with lots of people and lots of talk.

And (during those frigid days after Louis's death) it was as if a glass dome descended on me. Though I couldn't feel, I could move. I went through the motions of hostessing. I greeted people at the door, answered the phone, sat and talked and wept and talked. I kept a Kleenex box with me. I was amazed that I didn't cry all the time.

In between visitors, my minister and I planned the funeral. I selected pallbearers, I asked friends to sing, I chose music—marveling all the while that I could do these things.

On Monday, mail started coming. Stacks and stacks and stacks of mail—most of it from people I didn't know. But it was from people who had read my newspaper column for years and felt as if, in losing Louis, they had lost a treasured friend.

I was inexpressibly moved to discover how many people cared and wept and prayed— and then found a stamp.

And it was during this time that I discovered many of the opinions I'd firmly held about death went a'glimmering.

Many years ago when I was in college, I'd read Jessica Mitford's book, *The American Way of Death*. It was such a disgusting detailing of funeral practices that I vowed I'd never get caught up in them. As a matter of fact, I'd told Louis that, when I died, I just wanted to be bundled up in an orange crate, hauled out to the cemetery in our minister's station wagon and dropped in a hole. No ceremony. No nothing.

But, when I was face-to-face with death, I discovered the value of many of the practices I'd once abhorred. When I went up to the funeral home the morning of the visitation and saw my husband's body lying in the casket (yes, and gingerly touched his face when no one was looking—I never dreamed it would be so cold) I was mildly surprised that I decided to keep the lid open.

It was so obvious that it wasn't my husband lying there. The man I loved was eternities away from that place, and I felt very strongly that I wanted people to realize it.

During my callow, ignorant adolescence, I had felt that all the traditions surrounding death were barbaric. I didn't understand the people, the visitation, the food, the flowers, the cards.

How wrong I was. People filled our house from that first awful evening of the day he died. They bore the funeral meats—and wood. The food and fire they brought were symbols that life would, indeed, continue. But mostly, they were symbols of a need to share, to uphold, to comfort.

One of Louis's teaching colleagues sent a bouquet of yellow roses to the house—it was on the mantelpiece when we arrived home the night of his death. The card read, "I know this won't help, but..."

It was an instinctive sensitivity to the fact that all gifts seem paltry in the face of such overwhelming loss—that nothing can compensate. But people need to try. The curious thing about these symbols is, though they don't compensate for loss, they do declare life and love on the part of the giver. *They don't ease death, but they do affirm life.*

My family went up to the visitation at the funeral home—and my father was totally undone. He was moved, not only because of Louis's death, but because of the people who cared for him. They came through that cold, black night from hundreds of miles around— from three states, people came.

In the midst of her grief, Louis's mother found joy that so many of his students and former students came. Parents of students Louis had helped came. Column readers who knew him because I wrote so often of him came. And the very presence of so many loving, living people at the visitation was another affirmation of life. I didn't realize it then, but I did later. The good which people do lives long after the doing.

Before I lost Louis, I'd always felt awkward trying to tell someone I was sorry for their loss. I knew my feeble words could never comfort, never console, never compensate—and the bereaved would probably much rather I walk away.

But I learned. Don't walk away. Anything—anything you say is not only acceptable, it is welcomed. Words *do* comfort. Words *do* sustain. Don't be afraid to hold those who mourn. Don't be afraid to cry with them. It will do you all good.

For there is a curious inversion about comfort and grief, and I discovered it at the visitation. People came to comfort me, but I ended up trying to comfort them.

Although it may seem (to the unobservant eye) that the bereaved receive comfort, the contrary is true. The bereaved must give comfort. At least, I tried to. I somehow felt that, in receiving their love, I wanted to give them love—to say something to them about their impact and influence on our family's life. So, between weeping and hugging, I talked and chatted and introduced my mother-in-law and father and brother to our friends. Again, I'm not sure that this was proper or expected or even necessary. But that's what I did.

Flowers and plants had ever been a joy to Louis and me. I was unutterably touched by the tributes that flanked his casket. There were flowers from our farm neighbors; from Louis's students; from colleagues and friends and associates; from people I'd never met.

The cards and letters that arrived at our house were astounding. My father sat by the fire and read them, tears running down his face. "I never knew Louis was so important to this community!" he kept saying. "I never knew you were."

And the money. I had never known that people sent money. What a sensitive and sensible thing to do. Almost every card had several dollars in it. Many of them said, "Use this as you need it now. Don't save it for a memorial." Memorial? I hadn't even thought of that. But I was already in a money crunch, and my angry prayers to my unfeeling God dealt with supporting my family.

For years I'd joked that if I had a nickel for every card I'd never sent, I'd be a rich woman. Somehow, I just couldn't discipline myself to buy a card, write a note, look up an address and send something which I was convinced brought no joy in the face of grief.

How I wish I'd sent them! The letters and notes and sharings mean more to the bereaved than words can express. They are givings of self and of sorrow that will help keep happy memories alive.

In short, all the ceremonies surrounding the greatest watershed in life—death—are there because, throughout the centuries, they have helped. The things that don't help never last long enough to become traditions.

***

The day of the funeral was bright and cold—bone-breaking cold. It was held in our little Methodist church up in the village. I wanted it there instead of in the funeral home. We'd attended that church for almost twenty years. Our church family knew us.

Ever since we'd been married, Louis and I had remarked ruefully that it was a shame we'd selected such gorgeous music for our wedding, and then couldn't hear it because we were standing out in the narthex. So, for his funeral, I arranged that our family would be seated before the music began.

The simple grey coffin was in front of the church, closed. There was a wreath of evergreen laid on it. That was all.

We walked in—our daughters, his mother, my father and brother and I. The congregation sang one of Louis's favorite old Gospel hymns, *Shall We Gather at the River?* One of my closest friends (who'd been at the house to comfort us the night Louis died) sang *Amazing Grace*. The young - man - with - the - damper - closed sang *The Old Rugged Cross*. His voice broke on the last note.

One of Louis's colleagues, the high school music director, had organized not only the current choir, but many people who had sung in the chorus years before. They filled the church balcony, and sang *How Lovely Is Thy Dwelling Place* from the Brahms *Requiem*.

And our minister gave us Louis—a quiet, appreciative, peace-loving man. He knew him well.

***

There's a little, white, country church just up the road from our house, at Morseville Corners. It's only open for services twice a year. My husband had helped research its history for Heritage League; one hot August day, our whole family had helped catalog the tombstones and then we picnicked under the great old sheltering pines; we'd all helped paint the building and, for years, we'd all gone to the services.

The ancient cemetery in the churchyard looks out over the hills and the land that my husband loved. We buried him there. It seemed right.

And then we drove home—down the snow-packed gravel. Dusk lengthened across the purple snow banks as we pulled into our yard. I came into the house, built up the fire and huddled beside it, silent.

Up at Morseville, the pines creaked in the wind, their branches weighted down with snow.

And I knew I'd never be warm again.

CHAPTER TWO
THE BEGINNING

And then came the hard part. Living. Death was much easier than life. Living was so ugly, and death was so attractive, that I (again) seriously considered my own death. But this time (seeing that God was so inhuman as to deny me death) I would handle it myself.

This is not an easy thing to write, nor am I proud of it. I only tell you it because it does seem to be a course considered by many survivors. For this reason, I feel it's important.

I was driving up the highway to the village, starting the endless round of tedium that fills a survivor's life. I was trying to find money. My soul was as gray and as cold and as bleak as the day.

A great, orange, township dump truck, loaded with gravel, pulled onto the highway in front of me. The driver had been out sanding icy country roads. And I thought, "If I jam the accelerator down to the floor, I can crash into the back of that truck and go home to Louis."

And my knee tensed. And my hands gripped the wheel. And I couldn't do it.

I burst into tears—not because I had considered suicide, but because I seemed doomed to live out a life of barren emptiness.

I have since talked with widows who had the same desire for death. Each woman felt she was the only person who ever felt this, and that it was a terrible, unforgivable sin. One woman thought she was going mad until she discovered I'd had the same feelings, and survived them. Her fear of insanity had added immeasurable—and unnecessary—pain to her grief. I learned two important lessons that frozen morning, with the great, orange dump truck rumbling along ahead of me. I learned that God understands this feeling, and I learned that my life force is too strong to submit to the death wish.

***

Even now, as I write this, the physical memory of that desolation overwhelms me, and I experience once again the lassitude, the sluggishness, the inability to move that filled those exhausted days.

I could (after a fashion) drive and walk and cook and carry wood and shovel snow. But I couldn't focus on things like telephone books. My eyes and my mind and my fingers couldn't coordinate. Although they reconnected themselves within a month or two, I was still unable to read an entire book for well over a year. I had no attention-span for things unrelated to my loss.

***

The funeral director knew all about a survivor's problems with coordination. He typed out a list of the places I should go to try to find money. They were all located in the next largest city, some twenty miles from our village.

A young friend offered to go with me on my money search. Years before, she had been our children's baby sitter. Our children grew up and baby-sat for her children. In the process, we became very close.

The incident of the dump truck occurred as I was driving to town to pick her up.

Shaken and weepy, I drove us into the

city. Thank God I wasn't alone, for it was a disastrous day.

I walked numbly into the Social Security Office and was told that, very probably, there would be no help there. It didn't look as if my husband had paid enough into the fund.

We went to the Veteran's Office and no one was there.

We went to the insurance office and the file had been lost.

We went to a restaurant and, sitting in the car in the parking lot, threw our arms around each other and cried.

And then she took me out to lunch.

***

Oh, how important my friends were during those months following Louis's death! I don't know, to this hour, if they entered into a support-pact with each other, but I do know that not a day passed without one or two or several of them showing up. And calling. And praying.

One of the grimmest parts of the day for me was what I call the "crack". It was that time in late afternoon when I was through with the day's activities, supper was on the stove, and Louis was due home from school. He always came stomping in with an armload of wood and a cold nose. After he'd drop the wood, I'd run my arms around him under his coat and kiss him hello.

I dreaded the aloneness of that time of day, but, in the months after he died, someone always showed up in the crack. Someone always came and sat by the fire and listened to me read notes and cards aloud. Someone always talked to the girls and, surreptitiously, checked to see if I was fixing a decent dinner. (I know now that they were as worried about my inability to help my daughters as they were about me.)

My father phoned, long distance, in the crack of every day for over a year(!). My daughters' former baby-sitter ran "bed check" every night—rang up just to see what my plans were for the coming day.

The women who were at the house the night Louis died, plus many of the people who had gone to the retreat, continued to support throughout the coming months.

The young-man-with-the-damper-closed came over frequently, to carry in wood and sit by the fire. Neighbors and friends snowmobiled down to haul wood and shovel snow.

Friends and acquaintances (some of them given to me only for that period in my life) scooped me up with lunching and dining and shopping and phoning and meetings.

One of my biggest supports was the woman who drove us down that frozen highway the night of Louis's death. She was there at any hour of the day or night (either in person or at the other end of a phone line) to let me snuffle in her ear. She also combines great spiritual wisdom with incredible human perception and, during those days when I knew God had forgotten me, she was His person-in-place in my life.

God moved people into my days who filled a need then, and whom I rarely see now. One woman insisted I go to a concert with her just three days after the funeral. Others invited me out to dinners or to plays or to open houses or to Chicago.

And I was amazed that I could do all these things. I felt as if I were floundering through a vacuum-vat of cold molasses. Every physical movement seemed to take aeons. I would much rather have left the world to get on without me, but the world (in the form of my friends) kept pulling at me.

I was also amazed at some of the things that didn't hurt. It didn't hurt to hear other women talk about their husbands. I thought it would.

It didn't hurt to see other women with

their men. I thought it would.

It didn't hurt to talk about Louis. I thought it would.

And my friends saw to it that I did hear, that I did see, that I did talk. Somehow, they sensed that I needed to move within my vacuum-vat or I would shrivel and dry.

But though I yearned to, I knew I wouldn't shrivel and dry. The pain was too great. I was amazed at the actual physical pain of grief. The center of my chest felt as if it had been kicked by a horse—severe, localized, broken-hearted pain.

So I dressed my torpid body and made-up my frozen face and did all that was presented to me. And I marveled that someone so dead could move.

CHAPTER THREE
WRITE IS RIGHT

Even if friends and family hadn't combined in loving conspiracy to "Pull Lucy Through", I had much to do.

I continued to write my weekly newspaper columns. For years, I'd told my readers of our life as a family. Even though we no longer had a husband and father, we were still a family. So—the day after the funeral—I wrote a column. I didn't know what else to do. Meeting deadlines is absolutely ingrained in me.

Besides, we needed the money.

I also spoke. Less than a week after

Louis's funeral, I gave a speech to a large number of ladies at an elegant country club. For years I'd been entertaining people at conventions and meetings and banquets, and I couldn't disappoint all those program chairpeople.

Besides, we needed the money.

I also read cards and letters. Each night after supper, I built up the fire in the library. While the girls did their homework, I opened the armloads of letters that arrived every day.

I read every one. I wept over them. I shared them with my father when he called, with my daughters, with whomever dropped by. I couldn't get enough of talking about Louis—and of hearing what his life had meant to others.

I also wrote thank-you notes. I was brought up to write thank-you notes. My parents taught that, if someone was nice enough to give you something or do something for you, the least you could do was write and say "thank-you". Writing thank-you notes is as ingrained as meeting deadlines.

And I tried. I truly tried.

I wrote my heartfelt thanks to everyone who participated in the funeral, and to everyone who brought food and sent flowers. And I wrote thank-you notes to everyone who sent money, either for everyday expenses or for a memorial.

(I used the memorial money just the way Louis would have wanted me to. He was slightly jaundiced about charitable moneys being used for administration. Every year, when our church took up a Thanksgiving collection of food for a boys' home, he was enthusiastic. "That's the way to do it," he said. "We give a can of food—they eat a can of food." After he died, my minister and I borrowed a pickup truck, drove to a wholesale market and spent every dime of that memorial money on food. Then we drove fifty miles to the boys' home. The kids lined up bucket-brigade-fashion, and whisked the food from pickup to pantry in half-an-hour. Louis would have loved it.)

But eventually, grocery sacks full of mail mounted up the library wall. I lay this, in part, to the affection our friends felt for our family. But it is also true that hundreds of letters came from people who knew our family only through my newspaper columns.

It still humbles me to think of the number of people who wrote to us—for most of the letters were thoughtfully addressed not only to me, but to our daughters. And that meant so much to them.

But after the first several hundred letters were answered, I discovered I could no longer keep up with the mail. Not only could I not afford the postage—I simply didn't have the strength.

So I wrote a "Thank-You Note" column.

***

Sunday, March 19, 1979

TO THE WIDOWS: Thank you for sharing with me—for trying to help me through our mutual night. Thank you for your tears. Thank you for your prayers. God send you joy, my dear sisters.

TO THOSE WHO HAVE LOST CHILDREN: I can't fathom the depth of your grief at losing your child. Such promise, such hope. . .gone. I only know that, because you reached out of your own sorrow into mine, we were both blessed.

TO THOSE WHO HAVE LOST PARENTS: I know. I know. How I miss my mother. But do accept, in your marrow, that the very parent whom you mourn rejoices in the person you have become.

TO THE MEN: Thank you for reading. Thank you for writing. I once thought my husband was the only man who cared about these writings. You give me joy that you, too, care.

TO THE WIVES: I don't have to tell you to love him, do I? I know that (when you learned of my loss) you snuggled a little closer to your husband that night. Maybe you even surprised him with the depth of your gratitude that he was there, to snuggle. Death gives a momentary awareness of the impermanence of things—especially the good things. (The bad things seem to hang on forever.)

But alarm clocks and fuel bills and bologna sandwiches overlay that awareness, until you're right back in the old routine. You assume that, because you and he are together today, you'll be together tomorrow.

Tell him you love him lots. Tell him now. Tell him often. Tell him again. It's the one phrase in our marriage I never tired of saying—or hearing.

TO THE HUSBANDS: He who has eyes to see, let him see. He who has lips to speak, let him speak.

TO THOSE WHO FEAR: The night of Louis's death, when the girls and I slogged home through that black snow, one of my friends, with tears streaming down her face, flung her arms around me and said brokenly, "Oh, Lucy, I'm so afraid. I don't know what I'd do if I lost my husband. I don't know how I'd handle it!"

I have learned one thing. You don't have to know how you'd handle it. I am reminded of Corrie ten Boom's book, *The Hiding Place*. It is the story of a Christian family in the Netherlands, hiding Jews from the Nazis during World War II.

Corrie was very close to her father, and feared his dying. "I need you," she sobbed. "You can't die! You can't!"

"Corrie," he began gently, "when you and I go to Amsterdam—when do I give you your ticket?"

"Why, just before we get on the train."

"Exactly. And our wise Father in heaven knows when we're going to need things, too. Don't run out ahead of Him, Corrie. When the time comes that some of us will have to die, you will look into your heart and find the strength you need—just in time." *(The Hiding Place;* Corrie ten Boom with John and Elizabeth Sherrill; Chosen Books, Chappaqua, NY)

So don't worry about what you would do if you must enter into suffering. Being aware of the impermanence of life should only make you love more, touch more, bake more pineapple upside-down cakes.

And trust in God. He will give you the ticket when

you get on the train. He gave it to me.

TO OUR STOCKTON FAMILY: Louis and I used to say, somewhat wistfully, that we'd always be newcomers to Stockton—that because our family didn't stretch back five generations, we'd always be "those city folk down t'Morseville."

We were wrong.

Long ago, you made us part of your family. You gave us work, you educated our children, you taught us to worship, you came to dinner, you shared your perennials, you had us up, over, in and out.

The girls and I sat in front of the fireplace that cold night when Louis died. We decided then we'd have to be willing to move, if God has blessings for us elsewhere.

For the time being, at least, there is no greater blessing for us than right here.

One of our warmest friends, who is also my attorney, put it this way. "The only two lasting legacies you can leave your family are roots and wings."

Dear family, you have given us roots. We'll wait a while for the wings.

CHAPTER FOUR
THE GUILTIES

All those things I did—writing columns, making speeches, answering mail—were an important part of grief work. Forcing yourself to respond to the courteous conventions; forcing yourself to honor commitments; forcing yourself to continue playing out the charade of life ultimately makes that life real.

I learned about grief work because, although I lost my attention span and was unable to read for recreation until long after my husband's death, I did read. Many people sent me books, hoping to help me in my grief. I

gulped them down in frantic desperation—
hoping, praying, *willing* them to give me some
ease for my pain. Not only did they give me no
ease—they gave me greater cause for concern.
For I didn't seem to be dealing with grief in the
prescribed manner.

There are several stages of grief and, one
afternoon, I whipped through five of them in
fifteen minutes.

The first stage I call the "Guilties" and
there are three components.

Guilt Component A was that I blamed
myself for my husband's death.

Louis had never had heart trouble—no
history of anything. But he did have a slightly
high cholesterol count and I cooked accord-
ingly—corn oil, salads, fish and chicken, the
lot. During Christmas, however, I had
splurged. I made all the things he loved—
Scotch shortbread and Italian biscotta and
venison mincemeat pie.

"Oh, God!" I sobbed on my knees by our
bed. "Oh, God, what did I do?!" (As you can see,
my anger at Him did not mean I was quit with
Him. I needed Him around to shout at.)

"What if I hadn't cooked with butter?
Would he be alive now? I killed him. I know I
killed him. Oh, God!"

Guilt Component B was that I blamed

myself because I didn't save him.

"Oh, God, what if we hadn't gone to the retreat! If I'd been home, maybe I could have gotten him up to the doctor quicker. He'd be alive now. I could have saved him. I know I could have saved him. Oh, God!"

Guilt Component C was that I hadn't loved my husband perfectly and tenderly and unselfishly during the nineteen years of our marriage.

"Oh, God, the times we fought about money—and the children—and money—and the children. If I only hadn't been so extravagant—if I'd only been a better mother—if I'd only been a better wife—Oh, God!"

Although I had shut my bedroom door and buried my face in a pillow, my younger daughter awakened at the sounds of my sobbing. She ran into the bedroom.

"What's wrong, Mommy? What's wrong?"

I was so distraught I choked out my guilt that I hadn't been able to save Daddy.

With simple wisdom she said, "Oh, Mommy, do you think if you'd done all those things it would have mattered? If God wanted him?"

Her words were slaps in my sodden face. Whether or not it was truly God's timing for Louis, it still was not my place to have my daughter comfort me. If I persisted, the Guilties would ruin not only my life, but my daughters' lives.

I took her back to bed, kissed her and tucked her in, checked on my elder daughter and went into my room.

There, I had to deal with *Guilt Component 3* (the "why wasn't I perfect" syndrome) without my daughter's help. All the times I failed my husband came to mind. All the angry words and the hurt feelings and the petty selfishnesses presented themselves.

Alas, I hadn't been the perfect wife. There *had* been anger and hurt and selfishness in our marriage.

"So what!" I finally decided—with a little help from the Lord. Nobody is perfect in his relationships with everybody all the time. That's life. When we must, we ask forgiveness—from the one offended and from the Lord.

My husband wasn't much for my saying, "I'm sorry." He wanted proof. So, over the years, I baked a lot of pineapple upside-down cakes. As for the Lord—well, over the years, I've done a lot of knee-time.

I pulled up the comforter, wiped my face and started *imaging*. Not imagining, but *imaging*. I deliberately created in my mind an image of a closet with a sliding door. I pictured myself in front of it. I put all my Guilties about Louis's death in a big cardboard box, folded down the cover, picked it up and—straining with the weight of it—lifted it onto the closet shelf. Then I shoved it way into the back corner and slid the door shut. And I walked away from it.

And I haven't opened that door since.

It takes a conscious effort of will, putting away the Guilties. Even though we feel we're guilty; even though we know we're guilty; even though we *are* guilty, it is absolutely vital to put them away.

The Guilties won't do you or your family or your friends one bit of good. They certainly won't bring back the dead, and they can wreck lives. So, for the Guilties I say, "Shove 'em."

If you are a woman reading these words, this could happen to you. As a matter of fact, it will happen to over 60% of you. Somehow, you will lose a man—through death or divorce or desire or desertion. And, to a woman, you will get the Guilties. They come with Satan's sterile territory.

Don't buy them. With a conscious effort of will, put them away. They'll keep you from getting on with your life and, however desolate that life seems to you now, it *is* worth getting on with.

***

But I've got to be honest with you. A box full of Guilties that I've never been able to keep up on the closet shelf is filled with my failures with my daughters. Children Guilties.

I didn't even know I'd failed them until two years after Louis's death. That is when my own healing had progressed to a point where I could honestly care about their healing.

But I did fail them. And my awareness of that is bitter and rank. They (bless their forgiving hearts) insist I didn't. But I wish I'd been wiser with them.

I guess I did some things right. We talked about Daddy. We wondered what he'd have done in a particular situation. We daydreamed about our futures. We even, one night, sat and wrote down our dearest desires, to see if God was listening.

(I found that paper the other day. My senior in high school wanted a car. My junior in high school wanted to go to Europe. I wanted speaking engagements. And they both wanted me to get married again.)

We did many things together after their Daddy died. We flew to New York to see my father, we went shopping, we went out to dinner. We had parties. We planted gardens.

I hoped that activity would fill their lives, but they had fears I never imagined.

One late night I trudged upstairs and heard my younger daughter sobbing as if her heart had cracked. I ran into her bedroom, snapped on the light and gathered her in my arms.

"What is it, honey? What's wrong?! Are you missing Daddy?"

"Oh, Mommy!" She was racked afresh with tears. "Oh, Mommy—what if you die, too!"

I was aghast. I had never anticipated this. I had no idea that (in addition to the painful realities of our loss) my children were terrified of an existence without anyone to care for them. (I have since learned that this is a common fear among children who have lost one parent.)

I hugged her closer and we rocked back and forth.

"Oh, honey," I cried. "I'm going to be around forever. I'm too mean to die. You'll see. I'll be nagging you till you're eighty."

She smiled a quavery smile. And I hugged her tight. And then I tucked her in, kissed her, and turned out the light—just like when she was a little girl.

(I tucked both girls in, every night, until

they left home. We all needed close, physical contact—touching, hugging, loving. For those few moments in the cold, we were almost warm.)

I was terribly concerned about my elder daughter, for she had never really cried since the day her Daddy died. She's a very private person—much more so than her sister or her mother. In fact, she's rather like her father in that respect. She also is very tender of my feelings and (rather than tell me something that will hurt me) will gloss over it.

One night I tried to get her to talk about her feelings—her reactions towards how her life was proceeding since the funeral. She did her usual, evasive, don't-worry-mother number, but I kept pushing and picking and prying. Finally, she got so mad the tears came.

She cried and cried—first in anger and then in grief. It was the best thing she could have done. But I hated having to blast her into tears through rage.

In spite of those few times when I think I may have helped my daughters, I can't see that I was much emotional support or buttress at all. My own grief was so encompassing and enervating that I had little energy left to deal with theirs.

***

My elder daughter graduated from high school five months after her father died. She went on to college—in her very own car, by the way. That left my younger daughter and me, at home together.

She did a lot of growing up the second year after Louis died, for I was still running. I attended meetings all over the state, I went to Florida as the guest of an old friend, I did everything I could to avoid being home.

She had a cold, lonely, solitary time of it. She says now that it was good for her—it prepared her to cope with the loneliness she encountered when she studied abroad.

(When she graduated from high school, she studied in Luxembourg for a year and, after entering college, studied in Italy for another year.)

***

I did the best I could. My best may not have been good enough, but it was all I could come up with at the time.

I just wish I could shove these Children Guilties onto that overloaded closet shelf—and keep them there.

CHAPTER FIVE
THE ANGRIES

I got over the Guilties very rapidly. I did, however, have a longer run at the second stage of grief—the "Angries".

I really couldn't understand God. How could He let this happen! There He is, in the marriage business, with marriages failing all around Him. And here was a marriage that was working.

The last five years of our marriage were the most loving, the most secure, the most contented of them all. All my husband wanted to do was come home from work and sit by the fire with us. It sounds so corny, but the simple pleasures were the deep pleasures. He loved it when I played the piano and the girls sang duets. He loved having dinner guests at a table laden with food we'd grown and preserved ourselves.

We had so many mutual delights. We both enjoyed auctions and antique-ing. We both enjoyed entertaining and reading and talking. Neither of us liked watching televised football or baseball, so our evenings were spent together. He didn't like fishing or hunting and I didn't like bridge or teas, so our weekends were spent together.

We were so looking forward to getting the girls through college and out on their own, so we could do a little traveling together.

And now it was gone. Totally gone.

A dear friend came down two nights after the funeral. We sat in front of the fireplace and I got thoroughly ticked-off at God.

"Why did You give me so much—and then rip it away?!" I demanded angrily. "Over and over in your Word, You promise me joy. Well, there's precious little joy around here now!"

As far as I was concerned, God was absolutely untrustworthy. Would I always have the fear that I'd get zapped the instant things got good? How, then, could I ever enjoy the good—if there was good—which I doubted.

I sat and raged and cried. My friend sat and prayed and prayed. And I didn't get an answer.

And I still haven't gotten an answer.

And I don't think I'll get an answer until I reach the Throne.

But I did get something else. Something better.

Suddenly my sobs ceased. A quietness spread through my body like mist through the mountains, softening the sharp edges and the jagged peaks.

I got peace. On the very specific charges I hurled at God, He gave me peace. I don't ask those questions any more. I don't *need* to ask those questions any more. I simply don't care about the answers. Thank God.

And then I cried. Cried for Louis, cried for the girls, cried for me, cried for our loss. Good tears of grief—not frenzied tears of rage and betrayal.

And so I got over the Angries at God. What a relief. I hate being on the outs with a friend.

But I've wondered about that night— why I got that astounding and relieving peace. And I think it has to do with my faith.

Before Louis died, I had been minimally concerned about what would happen to my glib verbosity about my faith if I actually had to enter into suffering. After all, I'd been running around praising the Lord for five years and they'd been great years. I had good reason to praise the Lord. Oh, I assumed there was suffering around, but I was having a lovely ride.

And then suffering came. And my faith didn't move an inch. It didn't jiggle a jot. Even when I was having a good go at the Angries—when I was hurling stones at God—they were nevertheless flung from a solid foundation of faith in His existence—faith in His caring—faith in His love. I never doubted His presence—just His wisdom.

Ultimately, this faith glued my fractured universe together.

My reliance upon God—my faith—is an absolute gift. When Louis died I didn't need to sit down and say, "I've got to whomp me up some faith." It was there. And, with my sorrow, it deepened.

Someday you, too, may enter into suffering—if you haven't already. Somehow, sometime, a foundation wall in your life may be removed. If you haven't got a cornerstone of faith, your building may disintegrate. Don't wait for the trouble-times to come. Start building your house on solid rock. When the storm comes—and it will—though you'll be battered and drenched and shaken, you'll still be standing when it rumbles away into the past.

***

The Angries evince themselves in peculiar ways. Ancient rulers acted perfectly normally when they lopped off the heads of bearers of bad news. It wasn't reasonable. It wasn't logical. It was anger.

For years, I harbored unreasonable anger toward the woman who told me Louis was dead. I knew it was unjust and ignorant and ill-founded. But it was there. Time and prayer, thank God, dissipated it.

But this does happen. Sometimes our defense mechanisms aren't satisfied with railing away at the downright unnecessary waste of death. So we get angry at someone—anyone—for no good reason, except that we have Angries to vent.

I recently returned, with a friend, from his eighteen-year-old cousin's funeral. It was the stupid, senseless death of a bright, happy, popular, loving girl. And my friend was angry at me—for miles.

I finally figured out he wasn't angry at me—he was angry at Death.

***

There is another facet to the Angries. Frequently survivors get angry at the person who died—for dying and leaving them in this mess. The only time I got simply furious at Louis occurred a year-and-a-half after he died. Someone fixed me up with a blind date.

There was nothing wrong with the man. There was nothing wrong with me. But it was awful. I am too old to be a teenager.

I knew the minute we met that the evening would be two months long. So did he. Nevertheless, we played out our parts—though I did order only a salad because eating a full-course dinner would have taken longer.

When I finally got home, I experienced such resentment, such anger, such fury at Louis that I stomped into the house, flung my coat on the floor and slung my purse on the table.

"Dammitall!" I shouted. "I shouldn't have to be going through this garbage again! I'm too old to play get-acquainted games! You *knew* me! I *knew* you! And we were OK. Why did you leave me to this! Why! *Why!*"

And then I cried.

And then I laughed.

And then I went to bed.

CHAPTER SIX
THE CRAZIES

It was the second of the awful winters. It snowed remorselessly, just like the first. I dreaded looking out the windows. There couldn't possibly be any snow left to fall, could there? There was.

It snowed. Oh, how it snowed. The snow became a focus of grief. Every morning I stumbled around the kitchen, cooking oatmeal and begging for no snow. (That was one of the few prayers God ignored.)

I hated our adored Hill House. I couldn't bear sitting by the fire alone without Louis.

I got a terrible case of the "Crazies".

(Many grief-stricken people do. They develop behavior totally contrary to their normal selves. I have heard of widows desperately seeking solace in a series of unsatisfying physical relationships; desperately seeking money by writing begging letters to wealthy strangers; desperately seeking release by sleeping all day and refusing to leave the house.)

My Crazies?

I took up disco dancing.

A musician friend asked me to take a dance class at the YWCA with him. He wanted to learn new steps for his high school swing choir. It was a butterfly whirl from the "Y" gym to the local disco scene, and, while there, I found momentary oblivion.

I loved disco dancing! I loved the fancy steps that made me feel like Ginger Rogers. I loved swishy skirts and loud music and flashing lights and lots of people.

My friend soon learned enough steps to teach his choir, so he stopped dancing. But I was hooked. I went dancing four nights a week.

Disco dancing was hard, sweaty work and it proved an anodyne to my pain. I drove home over snow-packed roads into the glacial night and fell into bed, exhausted.

I always danced on week-nights—never

on weekends. Weekends are for couples. Singles swing during the week. I met a lot of young people who included me in their revels. One young woman even asked me to go dancing with her husband while she was away on a business trip. We both enjoyed it, and she knew I was "safe".

I'm not particularly proud of this phase of my Crazies. But I'm not ashamed of it, either. The people I met (with whom I had nothing in common but dancing) were first bemused by my appearance on their turf. Then they were accepting and, finally, they were welcoming.

My disco phase lasted about as long as the disco fad did—some four or five months. But it felt good. At the end of it, I'd cracked out of a hard, constricting shell.

***

I also started playing racquetball with an acquaintance. And, when the roads thawed, I took up jogging.

Subconsciously, I was doing the right thing to conquer depression—or at least to abate it for a bit. Moving the body is the classic panacea for depression. It triggers "endorphins"—a chemical linkage in the brain that produces positive feelings. Like flipping on an electric light switch, I didn't pretend to understand it—just to use it.

All this activity was totally foreign to me. I do hard physical labor in the house and the garden and the wood lot but, basically, I am a tournament-class sitter.

But I couldn't sit alone by my fire—yet. I couldn't pick up a book and read—yet. I still haven't picked up the handcrafts that once gave me such pleasure. Solitude stifled and numbed and deadened and bored me

***

I couldn't bear to be alone. So I invented "layering". Layering is arranging as many interesting things to do with as many interesting people as possible in a 24-hour period. If I wasn't booked to give a program on a specific day, I scheduled an anaesthetizing round of events. I might go to town for coffee, go to Prayer Group, stop in at the furniture store to see a friend, drive down to visit my mother-in-law, play racquetball with yet another friend, go out to supper with her, go disco dancing and bring acquaintances home for apples and popcorn in front of the fire.

"Where," I hear you cry, "were your children?"

One was away at college, and the other

was so involved in high school activities that I spent many nights alone. And even when she was home, I couldn't bear to be there.

I didn't do right by her, but I was driven by my own grief. If I didn't have something outside the house to look forward to each evening, I slipped back into agony.

***

I changed. People who didn't know me personally, just professionally, thought I was coping—on top of my widowhood. People who knew me personally were all too aware that I was frantically running from the loneliness which splintered me into fragments.

I was both those women—coping and fragmented. People could say of me, "She really does depend on God."

And they could also say of me, "You say she's a Christian? You'd never prove it by her behavior! Imagine—disco dancing at her age!"

True—on both counts. At one moment I could say with all my heart, "Isn't God good! He's blessing me every moment!"

And at the very next moment I could say, "What's to become of me?! I'm too young to be a widow and too old to be a single! Where on earth am I going?! And who cares? Does God?"

***

Surprisingly, I had lots of "ups" during that first year. I traveled and entertained and was entertained and spoke and danced and did glitzy things in Chicago.

But then I plunged into pits with abrupt, heartstopping descents that left me shaking.

"Aha!" you say knowingly. "Classic manic-depressive!"

No. I wasn't a classic anything. I was just a widow, and all that volatility came with the territory.

I don't have any answers for the Crazies. I'm simply describing that particular stretch of road as I blundered along it.

It's up and down, my dears—up and down.

CHAPTER SEVEN
THE POVERTIES

Another facet of grief that needed working through was the "Poverties". Suddenly, not having two regular paychecks each month annihilated me. I think that, except for the actual physical missing of my husband, the Poverties were the most devastating of the grief stages.

I was left with a big, old, brick farmhouse, five acres in the country, oil bills, electric bills, insurance payments, automobile upkeep and two teenage daughters. Suddenly, the entire lot was my responsibility.

You see, I was spoiled. My husband

spoiled me royally and I loved it. I really liked being supported. Oh, I brought in some income from writing columns and giving speeches, but we used that money for "frosting"—theatre tickets and vacations and Christmas presents. During the years of my marriage, I frequently told anyone who'd listen that I was so glad that someone else was responsible for the light bill.

But now, suddenly, I was responsible not only for the frosting, but for the entire cake. I was terrified.

I got the most virulent case of Poverties known to woman. I turned into a chintzy cheap-o. Nothing escaped my notice—oil, lights, soap. You name it—I couldn't afford it.

I cadged rides, I didn't invite anyone to supper, I avoided taking my daughters to the doctor for routine examinations—and I got absolutely paranoid about toothpaste.

Somehow, that toothpaste tube became the symbol of my money fears. I started hollering at the girls to press it harder from the bottom and, if necessary, put the tube on the floor and step on it in order to get the last little squidge.

And here, again, is where my faith in God not only bailed me out, but lifted me up. My dear friend came down yet another night to sit by the fire with me. I had gotten up several schemes in my mind for supporting my family.

First, I knew they were hiring for the night shift at a factory up in the village. I thought maybe I could learn to work on an assembly line. But then I had a whole new brainstorm.

Since I had been left with five acres in the country I would, I said, plant the biggest garden since Eden. And then I'd peddle fresh vegetables all over northern Illinois.

Now, that's dumb. That's roughly equivalent to peddling oil to the Arabs. They all have their own.

(It is not unusual for new widows of my generation to consider doing the most physically fatiguing work imaginable in order to support their families. Younger women have much more experience and many more skills to bring to single support. But my total identity was being Mrs. Louis R. Miele. Now that I wasn't, I thought I was nobody. And nobodies wore woolen babushkas and dug turnips out of sodden fields with their hands.)

I was working up a pretty good Pity Party for myself when suddenly my friend said peremptorily, "Lucy! You are a daughter of the King! Nowhere in that Bible does He say He wants you grub out your life in penury. And everywhere He says He wants you to live in health and joy and prosperity!"

Well. That really interested me, because there was very little prosperity lying around Hill House.

And, in one of those rare flashes of Biblical insight, I remembered Jesus, trudging around Galilee, doing miracles right and left. People were walking and leaping and jumping for joy because of Him. They could see and hear and praise.

And He went back to His hometown—to Nazareth. And everybody said, "Oh, yeah, sure, Jesus. I remember him. Wasn't Joseph his father and—saaaay, wasn't there a little somethin' funny about his birth? Who, him? Do miracles?"

And He couldn't. Oh, He did a couple, just to keep His hand in, but for His friends, His relatives, the people He grew up with and who had known Him best—He couldn't do a thing. Because they didn't *expect* Him to. And He left that region, brokenhearted.

And from this I learned that God's ability to give is only limited by my ability to receive. If I *expect* Him to give, He will.

So I said to Him, "God? If You're the King and I'm Your daughter, do You know what that makes me? A princess. And I'd like to be treated like a princess—royally. I don't want to

have to pray up dimes at toll booths. I want to
have enough to fly with."

That doesn't mean that I prayed for gold
coins to rain out of the dining room chan-
delier—though that isn't a bad idea. But
strange things started happening.

An acquaintance said, "Lucy, if you get a
job, you'll have to work eight hours a day, won't
you?"

"Sure. Why?"

"Then why don't you consider driving to
Chicago, giving a program and driving home
an eight-hour day?"

She not only turned my thinking
around—she found auditions for me, drove me
to them, waited and applauded—and then took
me out for lunch. God used her materially in
my life.

And speaking invitations rained down
upon me—like gold coins. During the four
months after Louis died, I had more engagements than I'd had in the previous three
years. To this day, I never hang up the phone
after a program date is confirmed without
saying, "Thank You, Jesus." I know it is
straight from His hand.

What wonderful work! I get all dressed
up, go out to lovely luncheons and banquets,
stand up and talk and nobody interrupts me,

people laugh and clap—and I can support my family.

It sure beats the night shift on an assembly line.

***

But God also showed me something else about getting. It's called giving.

My fireplace friend was the first to show me that you can't out-give God—that whatever you give you will receive.

I had some real problems with the concept. I thought it sounded like button-pushing. Like, "I scratch Your back, God, and You'll scratch mine."

But, within three months of my husband's death, I visited a very old, very posh, very main-line Episcopal church in the East—not a place where one would traditionally expect to find back-scratching. From the homily, I learned that God delights in paradox. And one of His very favorite paradoxes is, "If you give, you'll get."

It's scriptural. You'll find it in Malachi, the last book in the Old Testament. In it, God talks to His people—the children of Israel—the people to whom He has said, "*You* are my people." And these are the people who have said, "*You* are our God."

And God is simply furious.

"...You have robbed me of the tithes and offering due to me!" He accuses. "...Bring all the tithes into the storehouse so that there will be food enough in my Temple; if you do, I will open up the windows of heaven for you and pour out a blessing so great you won't have room enough to take it in! Try it! Let me prove it to you!"(Malachi 3:8-10 TLB)

This is the only place in the Bible where God says it is all right to test Him. This is the only scriptural authority we have to say, "OK, Father. Prove it."

It is all right. It is scriptural. It is (if you will) kosher.

I have this picture of heaven in my mind. And up there is a great big warehouse (shaped like the quonset hut bowling alley up in the village) with L*U*C*Y***M*I*E*L*E written right across the front. And in it are all the things God wants to give me. Whenever I give in His name, and ask in His name, He gets in there with a huge grain scoop and shovels blessings out the window.

Of course, sometimes He puts a request on "back order". And sometimes it isn't in stock at all, and never will be.

But wouldn't it be awful if it were there, and I didn't ask for it? That's why I ask. Lots.

***

I learned several other things about giving and getting. For instance, I can't tip God. I can't bribe Him. I can't slip it under His door. The fact that I gave myself to Him *first* makes my other gifts acceptable to Him.

And I discovered something else. There is a cute little quip floating around that says, "God loveth a cheerful giver, but He accepteth from a grouch."

Unh unh.

God doth not accepteth from a grouch.

. . .*He who sows sparingly shall also reap sparingly; and he who sows bountifully shall also reap bountifully. Let each one do just as he has purposed in his heart; not grudgingly or under compulsion; for God loves a cheerful giver.* (II Corinthians 9:6-7; NASB)

God only receives what I want to give cheerfully. It could be a phone call or flowers or lunch. (It's easy to be cheerful about lunch.)

More often than not, however, it's money. And the first figure that pops into my head is the amount I should give. What do I think— that He doesn't have it all already? That He really needs offering plates to do His mighty works? The giving is for me, not for Him.

God really impressed this principle upon me a year after Louis died. Our church has a yearly giving called Harvest Ingathering. We are asked to give an extra amount to handle special needs, like a home for disabled children or a new furnace for the church or repairing the sound system. When I received my Harvest Ingathering letter, the figure $100.00 popped into my head.

I was dismayed. *"One hundred dollars, God? One hundred?"* I had never given so much at one whack in my whole life—and I wasn't sure I had it.

But the figure kept resurfacing until, finally, I felt really good about it.

"OK, God. One hundred dollars. I'm sure going to be interested to see what You shovel out of the window."

Two days after I wrote the check, I got a letter from a woman I'd been in a Bible Study with twenty-five years before. I hadn't seen or heard from her for years. Writing on the day I wrote the check, she invited me to her condo in Florida—ten days, complete with airfare. You can draw your own conclusions. I know what mine are.

Sometimes, the first figure is small—maybe only $5.00. And I think, "Golly, God, is that right? Is that enough? Wouldn't ten be better?" Then I remember the "First Figure Philosophy". And I give it—cheerfully.

Cheerful giving is a chance to show how much we love Him, by obeying Him. Shakespeare was right when he said the quality of mercy (giving) is twice blessed—it blesses him that gives and him that takes.

Do you know that delicious feeling you have when you have bought just the right present for just the right person? You can hardly wait till Christmas to watch him open it—it's going to be such fun to see his joy. And then he opens it. And he is speechless with rapture—it *is* just the right thing! And you both get blessed right out of your socks—you with giving and him with getting.

That's the way God wants us to give to Him, with just that joy and anticipation. And that's just the way He's going to receive it— gleefully—plus trying like mad to figure out how He can bless you twice as much the next time around.

But you only get this glee in giving when you give to someone you really know—someone whose taste you know—someone who is so intimate with you that you feel as he does— someone you love. That's why you must give yourself first to God. Then you will know in your bones what else you can give that will just tickle His buttons.

God is a promise-keeping God—a tell-

and-show God. What He says, He does. First, He tells us in His Word what He's going to do. Then He shows us in our lives.

I don't have all victories to report in my walk without Louis. Frankly, I was so concerned about money during the first year of my widowhood that I'd probably have married the first man who offered to pay my light bill.

But, although the "Daughter of the King" School of Economics doesn't get much credence on Wall Street, it's getting a big play on Morseville Road. God proves, over and over, packed down and overflowing—like packing brown sugar into a cup—that He *is* going to take care of me royally. Like a princess.

Why, He can even pay the light bill.

CHAPTER EIGHT
THE LONELIES

Then there are the "Lonelies". The long-term Lonelies. My husband and I spent a lot of time together. We enjoyed the same activities, and we had the same goals—family, house and garden.

A month after my husband died, it was time to exhume our tulip pots. (Early in the fall, we had buried nine pots in a bulb pit out by the tool shed, planning to force bloom.) So I asked the young woman who had been our daughters' baby-sitter and her husband to help me dig them out.

It was a cold, windy day when we crunched through the crusted snow to the bulb pit. They had brought a pick and shovel, and my friend's husband cheerfully hacked through eighteen inches of frozen dirt and three inches of frozen sand to uncover the pots.

As he carefully unearthed each one, my friend and I carried them into the house. I had the ninth pot in my hands when he said, "Lucy, do you want me to put this sand back in the pit for next fall?"

Suddenly my life stretched bleakly before me, as frigid as February. The bulb pit had been *our* project—my husband's and mine. It was one of our mutual delights.

My words froze in my throat. "Oh—no—I won't ever be doing this again. Louis isn't here to do it with."

And I stumbled blindly into the house, clutching the pot.

When I came out, they were both furiously shoveling sand into the pit.

"Lucy," he said, stabbing at the heap. "We're going to fill it. Next fall, we'll do it together."

And the three of us, in the wind and the sand and the snow, put our arms around each other and wept.

***

Spring itself was even worse. As the perennial bed blazed into life, every tulip was a wound—every hyacinth a bruise. Spring's renewal withered me.

I don't mean it withered the "me" that planted onions or picked peonies or fixed supper or kissed the girls goodnight. I kept, albeit glacially, moving.

But the inner "me"—the "me" of my thought-life—withered for lack of communication.

There was much of spring that I wanted to share with my husband. One of the first things he noticed when we moved out to the country, years before, was the gradual reestablishment of the native red cedar trees. (They are trash trees—trees which are no earthly good to anyone. They spring up in hill pastures and look like thistles when they're small.)

For years, Louis had monitored their progress in self-reforestation. Somehow, it delighted him to see nature assert itself so cunningly.

One spring afternoon I was driving back into the hills to lead a Bible study. I drove by hill after hill almost completely covered with young red cedars. And I thought, "I must tell Louis they're really coming back. . ."

And then I remembered.

***

It was also a great joy for us to see pheasants gradually resuming their place in the natural scheme of things out here. For many years, farmers had hatched out pheasant chicks and set them free. And (as more and more land was set aside from cultivation) nesting habitat increased, and so did the birds.

Early on an April evening, I was driving down a country road on my way to give a program. There, in the middle of the road, was a cock pheasant. The circles of his red headfeathers blazed in the setting sun, and his iridescent greeny-blue neckfeathers glistened. His wings were taut, his tail erect. He was strutting and preening and proud.

I stopped and turned off the motor. I knew that somewhere on the verge of the road there had to be a little brown hen. Sure enough, she soon coquetted out onto the gravel.

She was so nonchalant, so insouciant, so oblivious of all that male glory manifested just for her! She picked around for a bit and then skipped back into the weeds. She was so subtle—and he was so dumb—that he lost her.

Down went the tail! In went the wings! All his proud cockiness dissolved as he scurried along the grassy bank, peering anxiously into the verdure. Finally, he just stopped still on the edge of the road, jerking his head from side to side, searching for her.

She saw that, if there was ever to be any progress in this affair, she'd have to take matters into her own wingtips. She slipped out of the weeds and came up behind him. Then she cleverly stretched forward and picked a bit of weedseed from right under his beak. Then, with a flirtatious flip, she flitted through the fence into the field.

Up came the tail! Out went the wings! And he strutted proudly after her.

I laughed out loud as I started the car. "Oh, I must tell Louis..."

And then I remembered.

***

My husband was always so interested in how his students turned out. Nothing pleased him more than to be stopped in the street by a young couple—the man carrying the baby— and to hear, "Remember me, Mr. Miele? I had you in sixth grade. This is my wife—and this is my son."

A charming young woman came up to me one evening after I'd given a program and said, "I had your husband in sixth grade."

"Oh, how nice," I replied. "What are you

doing now? Married? Working? Children?"

She shared for a bit and then I said, "Louis will be so glad when I tell him I met you..."

And then I remembered.

***

Louis always waited up for me when I was out at night on a speaking engagement. He wasn't always awake, but he was up, sitting in his chair by the fireplace. I would go into the library, bearing a plate of goodies from the refreshment table, and awaken him.

"How did it go?" he would ask as he munched on a brownie. "Were you fantastic in Freeport? Remarkable in Rockford? Sensational in Stillman Valley?"

He always wanted to hear about the program, the people, the laughter. As anyone in theatre will affirm, this afterglow is as important as applause.

One night I drove home from Belvidere. "Now, how will I tell him about the speech?" I mused. "That I was beautiful in Belvidere? I was blazing in Belvidere? They went bonkers in..."

And then I remembered.

***

I miss talking about our daughters. I

miss his steady response to the girls. I miss his helping to bear the awful and awesome burdens of parenting.

And how I miss sharing the triumphs. Both girls made the high school honor roll a month after he died and (when I read their names in the paper) I thought, "Louis will be so proud when I show this to him."

And then I remembered.

***

People thought that (because I do have a fairly visible life in my column) I was healing quickly.

Six months after the funeral, a friend asked me, "How are you doing, Lucy?"

"I'm lonely," I said truthfully. "Sunday afternoons and evenings when my daughters aren't home plunge me into despair."

"You?" she said incredulously. "You're lonely? I can't believe it."

"Why not?" I replied. "Louis just died six months ago."

"Yes, but you—*you—lonely?*"

I knew people wanted reassurance that I was recovering from the amputation. But I couldn't give it to them.

***

I never thought I'd live through the first

year. I couldn't escape the loneliness that enveloped me. I was so frightened of solitude that, as I told you, I spent a lot of time in discotheques.

But the Lonelies shredded me to bits, no matter how fast I danced.

***

The Lonelies abated with time. New experiences, new interests, new people all helped to fill my life. But even now, after all these years, I still miss Louis.

I miss his emptying the cat box and taking out the trash and bringing in the wood. I miss making him pineapple upside-down cakes and correcting his spelling papers. I miss sharing a footstool in front of the fire on Sunday afternoons, exchanging sections of the paper.

And I miss turning over at night and having him there.

CHAPTER NINE
THE FIRST YEAR

So there you have them—the Guilties, the Angries, the Crazies, the Poverties and the Lonelies.

They are all part of grief work.

Grief books use that phrase a lot. It sounds as if you wake up in the morning and say, "Well, I gotta get some grief work done today." Like defrosting the refrigerator.

But it's nothing you can plan to do. It just happens—mostly with tears. And it's hard work, too.

Grief work is, basically, realizing that

the life you had before is over. Totally over. Nothing again will ever be the same. This is not to say that your new life won't be beautiful or challenging or exciting or fulfilling. It will simply not be the same. And you have to rip away, or tear away, or shred away, all the tender, loving strands that bound you to the life you lost.

The shredding of these strands is painful. Agonizing. It takes a long time. The Victorians knew what they were talking about when they prescribed a year of mourning. It takes at least a year to work through the worst stages of grief. You have to experience alone all the things you shared together. The first Christmas, the first wedding anniversary, the first tulip—all these things you must do alone.

The black armbands Victorian mourners wore said to all who saw them, "This is not a whole person. This is a person who should be treated tenderly, gently, lovingly. This person should be coddled and cosseted, as you would coddle and cosset someone who has had major surgery."

For we, the survivors, have experienced a wrenching amputation. I literally felt as if two-thirds of the essential "me" was ripped away. I told you before that all I ever wanted to be was Mrs. Louis R. Miele. My husband was my ticket—my passport to the world. Because he loved me, I felt I had worth. Without him, I was worthless.

I know this is irrational, but survivors are not known for their rationality. I also know this is strange in this day-and-age, when women, more and more, are discovering how worthy they are in their own right.

Louis always encouraged and supported me in a number of non-traditional activities, like writing and speaking. And he saw work as something that needed doing, not something that needed to be done by one sex or the other. For instance, he always vacuumed the house for me and I always worked in the woodlot with him. But I (though only forty-two years old when Louis died) was the product of an earlier generation. The fact that he had never treated me chauvenistically made no difference to my sense of worthlessness.

A major source of concern for me was my inability to make decisions. At a time when I was called upon to make more long-lasting, far-reaching decisions than ever before in my life, I literally couldn't decide whether to phone someone, write someone, or forget the whole thing.

This was most distressing. For years, I've been known as decisive and opinionated. If you needed an opinion on anything, all you had to do was ask me. Frequently, you got it without asking. My opinion may not have been logical, well-reasoned, or even interesting. But it was *instant*.

During the first year of my widowhood, I wavered and vacillated and floated. I hated myself that way. But I couldn't do anything about it.

And I got heaven-sent help for my indecision.

A Bible-study friend asked who would be my "cover".

"My what?"

"Your cover. Louis was your cover—the one you went to for advice and protection. Now you need someone else. It's scriptural."

I'm still not sure if it is, but it's a marvelous idea, anyway. I asked the husband of my fireplace-sitting friend if the girls and I could come to him with our questions and problems. He said, "Yes,"—little dreaming the number of picayune decisions he'd have to make.

The first big question he faced was my bed. I was cold. Freezing. (That was the winter the windchill factor plummeted to -87 degrees.) Should I, I asked, invest in an electric mattress pad?

Bless his heart, he didn't laugh. He gave

it thoughtful consideration for all of three
seconds and then pronounced his opinion.
"Yes," he said. "That would be a good idea."

Over the intervening years, he has been
called upon to make more important
decisions—especially regarding my daughters.
But they are so convinced of his prayerful wisdom that, to this day, whenever they are faced
with a decision or a dilemma or both, they call
him. It can't have been easy, taking us on. But
what a continuing source of caring he is!

***

A funny little loss I noted immediately
was not having someone to perform the "cour-
tesies". My husband, for instance, always
helped me on with my coat—not just in public,
but every morning when we left the house.

He always walked on the outside, offering his arm for me to hold. I always hung on,
too—no matter what the weather. I just liked
touching him and he, it seemed, liked it too.

I miss that.

***

I also discovered that the ancients knew
whereof they spoke when they spoke of a
broken heart. I'd always thought the phrase
was poetic imagery. But it's true. I literally had
a broken heart. I was amazed at the actual

physical pain I felt, right in the middle of my chest.

These old-fashioned notions (a year of mourning and a broken heart) have lost much credence in modern society. But they are astonishingly accurate. We survivors must be forgiven if we behave irrationally, unlike our former selves. For we are *not* our former selves. And we never will be.

Society today gives the survivor about three months. And then it's, "Awcummon, lady. You weren't buried with your husband. Get on with your life."

It takes longer. Much longer.

***

I was truly blessed, during those first three months, by people who saw to it I was not alone. I have never, before nor since, had so much company. People plowed through blizzards to have tea by the fire, to take us to dinner, to just be with us. I knew, even as they happened, that the visits would taper off. People have their own lives to lead. But I was stronger because of them.

***

I also knew that, although I had two or three people I could talk to, they didn't understand what I was going through. They still had

their men around. Unless they personally
knew my appalling hollowness, they couldn't
really understand.

I told myself that I didn't want them to
have such a loss, just so they'd understand my
pain. But in my self-absorbed little heart-of-
hearts, I wondered if they'd be able to bear up
better than I could.

My friends were there—solidly, steadily,
sensitively—but in the wee, small hours of the
frosty mornings, God and I had to battle
through alone.

***

I coveted my friends' sensitivity toward
my loss. But I soon realized that I must also be
sensitive to them, and to other acquaintances.
Once people sympathized with me, I tried to
turn the talk to their lives—their children,
their jobs, their hobbies, their church work.

I'll tell you true—I didn't really *care*
about their lives. All I really cared about was
my death. All I really wanted was stroking and
salving and bandaging. (Actually, all I *really*
wanted was Louis. Failing that, I'd settle for
sensitivity.)

But I went through the motions. It was
good for me, and relief for my friends. It took
some time, but eventually I *was* interested in

them. It's another of those peculiar inversions—the action precedes the motivation. And (because I hadn't demanded their total obeisance to my loss) they were still around when my heart started beating again.

***

Being a survivor means having the starring role in life's greatest tragedy. The spotlight focuses on the survivor, for a while. Some survivors (I'm sorry to say) want to stay in the spotlight longer than necessary.

I am ineluctably reminded of these lines from Edward Lucie-Smith's poem, *The Lesson:*
". . . for there and then I knew
That grief has uses . . . All the other eyes
Were turned towards me.
Somewhere in myself
Pride, like a goldfish, flashed a sudden fin."

But, though grief doesn't abate quickly, we survivors cannot demand that others venerate it forever. After a bit, we must let them get on with their own starring roles. Alas, it takes at least a year before we can even begin to write new scripts for our own lives.

***

I was so relieved when I got through that first year. I'd made it through all the things Louis and I had done together—alone. I'd done all the things I'd always done—Valentine's dinner for Gramma, graduation party for our elder daughter, planting gardens and sharing flowers, huge feasts on Thanksgiving and Christmas—the lot. Plus I had given speeches and written columns and supported us.

And, with a sense of weary relief, I got through the anniversary of the day Louis died. I'd made it through the tough part, I thought. From now on, it had to be easier.

The very next night, for the first time since he died, I dreamed of Louis. I was walking up a mountain path. There were pine trees and birches beside the path. Their roots occasionally stretched across the trail. I looked up, and there was Louis, coming down the path toward me.

"I *knew* you weren't dead!" I cried. "I knew it. I *knew* it!"

He was so real. He was so alive. I experienced a rush of deliverance from my pain. Suddenly I felt whole again. Awareness and completeness and delight flooded through me. At last. I could start living. I could live. I could live!

And then I woke up. Agony clenched me. Tears poured from my eyes. Terrible wrenching sobs shook my body.

He was dead. I was dead. And I had to start over again.

CHAPTER TEN
A BREATH AT A TIME

Somehow, you work through grief. At the visitation, other widows sought to comfort me and said, knowingly, "Time heals, Lucy. Time heals."

And I thanked them for their sympathy and concern and presence, but inwardly I screamed, "How do I live through that time?!"

You live through it a breath at a time, a prayer at a time. One way I lived through it was by assuming an interest in other people until I ultimately became genuinely interested in them.

Another way was work. It somehow devolved that I could never indulge in my favorite form of escape—sleep. At a time in my life when all I wanted to do was crawl into bed, pull the covers over my head and leave the world to function without me, I had to get up, get my face on and get cracking. I resented this. My constant prayer—to support my family—was being answered. But I didn't want to have to *think*—to have to *do*. I wanted to sleep.

Sleep was freedom from pain. All day I yearned for it, though I knew it would be sporadic. For I awakened at various times during each night with with my left arm groping behind me, searching for Louis. Sometimes (when his absence was too hurtful) I called one of my friends on the telephone. But not often.

I courted sleep. I welcomed sleep. Even though I knew what would happen in the morning.

Every morning it happened the same way. I drifted up into that sleepy, half-dozing prelude to full awakening. I was conscious— but barely. I was drugged with sleep—drugged with forgetfulness. It was a "blank space"— devoid of feeling of any kind. And then, as I awoke, the pain hit me. It gripped me with renewed fervor, as if sleep merely invigorated it. Then it plunged with me into the pit again.

And I dragged myself out of bed, got the girls up, fixed breakfast, put on my face and started on my weary rounds.

As time—healing time—went on, the most obvious indication that my wound was healing was a consciousness of that blank space during the day. At first, it was so infinitesimal I hardly noticed it. I would be doing something—writing or cooking or driving—and, suddenly, I'd be overwhelmed with pain. Which meant that, for however short a period before, I had been *without* pain. I was so involved in something else that the grief abated, albeit briefly.

I started "clocking" these recurrences of pain, and they occurred more and more frequently. Which meant that I was without pain more and more frequently. It was a "good news/bad news" syndrome. The good news was that I was without pain occasionally. The bad news was that, when it returned, it was a fresh onslaught. It seemed to gather strength during its absence. At times it was so sharp, I almost yearned for the dull, continual, *familiar* ache.

***

There was also a curious, secret satisfaction in helping others through their losses.

Just three weeks after Louis died, one of his
pallbearers died in exactly the same way—a
sudden, massive heart attack. Less than an
hour after I heard of it, I walked into his
widow's home, my heart breaking for us both.

Friends later said to me, "Wasn't that
hard for you to do? To get up there so soon?"

It would have been harder *not* to go. It
was another inversion—another of the great
turnabouts God delights in. When you give
comfort, you receive it.

I cried for her. I cried for me. But there
was another element than mutual loss in my
tears. It took me awhile to identify it, and I
was amazed to discover how selfish it was.

The element was relief.

Much as I ached—for her and her family,
for me and our family—I was unaccountably
relieved. I was three weeks ahead of her into
my grief work—three weeks she had to crawl
over terrain I'd already crossed.

Never again do I have to hear that Louis
is dead. Never again do I have to go through
that first night alone. Never again do I have to
tell our daughters that their Daddy is dead.

I hurt for her and I hurt for me—but
never again need I know that awful desolation
of Louis's death.

Only three weeks into my widowhood

and I discovered that it is true. Time will heal. But as prisoners say, so say I from my solitary cell.

It's hard time, my dears. Hard time.

CHAPTER ELEVEN
FRIENDS: SILVER AND GOLD

Every woman who loses a man also loses some friends. First (and most painfully) you lose those who were friends because you were couples together. They simply don't know how to deal with a single person, for ours is truly a couple-oriented society.

As time moves on (and more and more people become single because of the aforementioned death, divorce, desire or desertion) everyone will have singles in their lives. Maybe, in twenty years or so, we will know how to handle society with singles. And we'll all be a little more accustomed to dealing with odd numbers. Right now, however, American society is in a carry-over from the old high-school-double-date patterning. Singles are still "odd people out".

***

You also lose friends who fear adding to your pain. "Do I talk about it? Don't I talk about it? What if she cries? What do I do then?"

Once the funeral is over and they've done all the things they know how to do (flowers, casseroles, phone answering), most people don't know how to do anything else.

"I'll wait a couple of months, till she's adjusted," they think. It is extremely uncomfortable to be with someone who is adjusting—who is doing grief work. And the person who grieves becomes a whole new person in the process. After a couple of months (if a friend isn't sharing the ongoing metamorphosis), friends become strangers.

***

There is also an awareness of the impermanence of their own marriages. By empathizing with you, your married friends are reminded that they, too, could suffer a similar loss. They subconsciously fear that death is contagious.

Cherish the friends who love you and pray you through your pain. It's painful for them, too.

***

You also lose friends who (quite frankly) think you have your eye on their men—or vice versa.

This is an uncomfortable phenomenon. Women who are recently single are considered fair game by many men. This is difficult—especially if a friend's husband offers to assuage your bereavement.

It's also difficult because you, probably, have some real questions about your femininity. You need reassurance that you are still desirable.

Your erstwhile friends don't tell you why they drop you. They may not even know why. But it underlies their behavior. They send flowers. They show up at the funeral. They invite you once or twice. And then they're gone.

It is very hard to deal with this. In addition to losing your husband, you are losing people you thought were friends. Loss is multiplied. I still miss some friends Louis and I had as a couple.

***

Because I felt I had my being only as a

wife, I was reluctant to do anything socially without a man. Again, this is part of my generation. We grew up thinking that "going out" meant going out with a man. If we went out alone or with another woman, it told the world that we couldn't get a man to take us.

But I discovered something as I moved on into widowhood. We women are a simply splendid sex! We also engage in wonderful dinner table conversation.

I have increasingly less sympathy for women who say, condescendingly, "I really get along better with men than with women." Pfui. Not only do they write off a possibly interesting evening with me, they write off a lot of interesting evenings with others.

Don't think you'll be conspicuous by going out with another woman or group of women. For once, society is working for us in this regard. It is no longer essential to have a man around to pick up the bill. It's nice, but it's not essential.

***

Many new acquaintances came into my life that first year. They were moved to take me to concerts, invite me to dinner, drive me to Chicago. Most of these relationships were short-term, but I was very grateful for them.

Those people helped me in specific, particular ways, and then moved on to help others.

***

Although I was numb, I was still aware of how many people were making an effort to include my daughters and me in their lives. I mentioned to the girls one night that I appreciated it, but we probably shouldn't get used to it. It might not last long.

My younger daughter said, "Mo-*ther!* Look at all the single friends you and Daddy had. What makes you think that you won't reap that harvest now?"

I'd not realized it before, but she was right. At the beginning of each school year, Louis always brought new, young teachers home for supper. Some of them stayed friends for years. We made weekend trips all over the midwest with older friends. We couldn't begin to celebrate Christmas without our elegant librarian friend and the girls' piano teacher.

I'd not thought of these people as single—just as friends. But I did reap the harvest.

***

I am continually delighted that a couple who were acquaintances when Louis died made the effort to become friends. They had to make it, because I had no energy to give to anything.

She is the world's definitive shopper and (less than a week after the funeral) she took me shopping. She forced me into a dressing room, forced me to try on clothes and forced me to buy two new dresses—on sale, naturally.

Though I didn't realize it at the time, that was one of the most thoughtful things she could have done. It was important to make a statement—to me, if to nobody else—that I would continue life. A new dress is an investment in the future. I had to hang around long enough to wear it.

This couple loves to lavish hospitality on people, and they are singularly free of the couple-oriented-mentality. Thus, I am invited to elegant affairs, casual dinners, family celebrations and intimate groupings because I'm me—not because I'm married.

***

If somebody—anybody—asks you to join them, do so. You won't feel like participating socially, but join in anyway. If you turn down invitations too often, pretty soon there won't be any. And be sure to reciprocate.

***

As I moved into genuinely caring about

other people and their problems, the Pity Party
was invented. It started out as a Porch Party. A
group of five women came down one hot August
night, we sat on the porch and (as the evening
progressed) we discovered that each of us had a
problem she couldn't solve.

One woman had children/school problems and didn't know whether to go to the
teacher (and thereby be a nagging mother) or
not go to the teacher (and thereby be a neglect-
ful mother).

Some of us had experienced similar
problems with school officialdom, and were
able give her practical advice which eased her
mind and gave her a course of action.

Another woman had severed a work
relationship and was at loose ends. Someone
said, "Let's work up a mailing list." The next
day, four of us set four typewriters on her
kitchen table and helped establish her own
business.

At irregular intervals since that long-ago
summer, one or the other of us will call up and
say, "Let's have a Pity Party." It is a clarion cry
for help, and we all respond instantly.

We sit around chatting, various problems arise, we spend maybe three minutes
pitying the afflicted one, and then someone
says briskly, "Well. What are we going to do

about it?"

Sometimes we laugh. Sometimes we cry. Sometimes we advise. Sometimes we type. Sometimes, just learning that someone has successfully covered the same ground helps us deal with the problem.

We have established perfect trust. Nothing we say goes beyond the porch or the fireplace or the kitchen table. It is a remarkable group—one which I treasure.

***

The young friend who was formerly baby-sitter for my daughters is a particular delight. It is unique that we have made the jump from mother/baby-sitter to sister/friend.

We see each other almost every day. We have an alternate-cycle relationship. When I'm down, she scoops me up. And I do the same for her. I don't know what we'll do if we ever hit the pit at the same time, but I imagine we'll cry. And then we'll laugh. And then (because she's an enthusiastic problem-solver) she'll figure some way to crawl out.

***

Since Louis died, I've been blessed with new friends. These are handsome, young couples with attractive, small children, who call me (to my delight) Auntie Lucy. These young couples take me out to supper, come down to supper, bring supper down or (when I cook too much for me) let me take supper there. They even sensitively determine when I might need lots of children vying for my attention, and invite me to stay overnight.

***

I treasure deeply my fireplace-sitting friend who counselled me so wisely those cold nights after Louis died. We are also blessed with perfect trust, for we can be totally honest with each other. We confess all our pettinesses and fault-findings and unloving observations to each other.

She is wonderfully uncritical. Once, after I'd confessed some particularly ridiculous bit of behavior, I asked her why she never slapped my wrist. "I've wondered that, too," she told me, "especially when you were going through your Crazies. But God said, 'I haven't called you to correct Lucy—just to love her.' Isn't God good? That's just what I want to do, anyway!"

We share our hopes and our disappointments. We talk about men and money and children. And then we pray together.

She is a continuing source of comfort and joy, for she is truly centered in the Lord. "If He be for us, Lucy, who can be against us!"

***

How grateful I am for the telephone. Sometimes (especially when I can't afford it) a long-distance call to an old friend is the best money I can spend.

One friendship stretches back to the third grade. My old girlhood chum loved Louis as much as she loves me. She wrote *Lucy's Song* when he died. She also scooped up our elder daughter when she went west to seek her fortune.

My Georgia friend sent her gorgeous son up to escort my elder daughter to her Senior Prom. My Wyoming friend finds Blue Willow ware for me, calls often and asks my (!) advice. My Waukegan friend shares her joy and her daughters. My Wilmette friend is always there in times of trouble.

To paraphrase Thomas Jefferson, "The tree of friendship must be refreshed from time to time with lavish applications of stamps and phone calls."

***

Years ago, my mother gave me two pieces of advice which have stood me in good stead.

"Never make all your friends in your own age group," she said frequently. "If you do, you'll end up with none. They'll all die at the same time."

I am truly blessed with friendships which span the years.

And I recall the other bit of maternal advice. It is a little verse she wrote in my limp-leather bound autograph book when I was very small. It's curious that I've remembered it all these years, but its wisdom has particular meaning for me during my life alone.

"Make new friends, but keep the old;
One is silver—the other gold."

CHAPTER TWELVE
MONEY MATTERS

When Louis died, I didn't know a T-Bill from a tennis ball. I thought Ginny Mae was Daisy Mae's sister, and M-1 was a main highway in England. In short, I knew nothing at all about money.

Not only had I never needed to know—we barely had enough money to pay our real estate tax—but I didn't want to know. I could afford to ignore money because we didn't have any.

But suddenly, I had a lump sum of money—Louis's insurance policy. It was more

money than I'd ever seen in my life. (In actual
fact, it was a pitiful pittance. When Louis and I
took it out, we thought we could live on it
forever when it matured).

It was too little to do anything with, and
too much to do nothing with. So I had to deal
with it—put it somewhere where it could earn
interest. I also had to sort out Teachers' Pen-
sion Funds, Social Security (yes, I finally did
get some money to help with the children),
Veterans' Administration Funds—in short,
every sort of form-filling.

I was in no mental shape to start learning a new vocabulary—I told you my attention
span went a'glimmering into the twilight for a
long time. But Louis and I had an old friend
who is (he insists) just a "simple country
lawyer". Which means he's very shrewd, very
smart, and very sweet. And he agreed to help
me.

He was—and still is—a blessing in my
life. In addition to being a smart lawyer, he has
an absolute compulsion to impart knowledge.
My appointments with him are as much
therapy as anything else, because our conver-
sations range from origins of words to yards of
Kipling to slightly salacious Latin limericks—
which he gleefully translates. Wonderful!

He has lavished hours on my financial

education. I'm just smart enough to tell him when I don't understand—and he keeps working with me until I do.

Thus have evolved the Three Commandments in dealing with lawyers. The first and great commandment is: *Don't be ashamed to admit you don't understand something. Keep asking until you do.*

And the second is like unto it: *If a lawyer continually talks in terms you don't understand—find another lawyer.*

And the last shall be first: *Find out the fees before a lawyer starts working with you.*

I haven't become a financial whiz, but I have learned that there's more to money than paying the bills.

***

Grief numbs the mind. At a time when I couldn't even think, I had to make more long-ranging financial decisions than ever before. It took over a year after Louis died to regain rational decision-making powers.

I won't even presume to advise you specifically on investments. *But I urge you to find someone who can—someone you can trust.* (It's nice, but not necessary, if he can quote Kipling.)

***

"DON'T ASSUME" AXIOMS

Don't assume that your banker will recommend anything but putting your money in his bank.

Don't assume an investment broker who made millions for a friend's uncle will do the same for you.

Don't assume stock-and-bond brokers have your best interests at heart.

Don't assume you can do hop-scotch real estate deals because you know someone who made a killing on gas stations that way—unless that someone is you.

These are all legitimate investments. But don't make them without personal knowledge and/or a trustworthy advisor. There are lots of people with lots of schemes out there, anxious and willing to handle your money.

You owe it to yourself and your children to search for good advice, and to educate yourself about Certificates of Deposit, Individual Retirement Accounts, Treasury Notes, Treasury Bills, and the price of gold. She who learns about interest earns it. She who doesn't learn about interest pays it.

***

If you have children and you can possibly keep it, don't sell the house during the first year of your loss. Don't move. Your children need stability. How I regret thrusting the possibility of moving at my daughters the night of Louis's death.

On the other hand, you may need to move immediately. If that is so, don't buy Guilties because of it. The very activity of moving will help strengthen you emotionally.

***

The first time I walked into my lawyer's office (less than a week after Louis died) he sat me down and said, "Lucy, I'm going to say something that you won't like. But I want you to hear it. You'll probably get married again— no, wait, let me finish—and if you do, I want you to promise me something. Before you even get the license, I want you to bring him down here to me so he can sign off on your property. If you died or you got divorced, it just wouldn't be right for him to take part of what you and Louis worked so hard for. That belongs to Louis's children."

I was sobbing by this time but (even in my distress) I recognized his wisdom. And I promised.

It is statistically unlikely that I will ever marry again, but you may. Do not remarry without a pre-nuptial agreement as to property. The law varies from state to state, but in Illinois (where I live) if my new husband moved into my house, I couldn't sell it without his signature on the deed. If I died, both he and my children would have rights to the property Louis and I had acquired. A pre-nuptial agreement assures this won't happen.

If your prospective mate doesn't want to sign one, think again.

Check the laws in your state. It's vital that you do all you can to preserve your children's heritage.

***

It's also important to decide how you are going to share household expenses—before you get married and find out he doesn't really want to pay the light bill. Again, a pre-nuptial agreement can help avoid some real hassles later on.

***

Louis and I did all the work in our house. We bashed out walls and laid brick walks and built cupboards. After we'd filled a crack or cobbled together bookcases or painted a wall, Louis always sat back, looked at it and said, "Well, it's not perfect. But it's better than it was."

We weren't handy, but we kept the place

alive.

For a year after Louis died, I didn't do a thing *for* the house—or *to* it. And a house built in 1857 needs constant repairs.

Two dear friends (a husband-and-wife team) needed work just at the time the house was about to fall down around my head. So I'd call them and tell them what new disaster had struck the house and then say, "Now, start praying for work for me."

They'd pray for work; I'd get a speaking engagement; they'd come down and fix the house; I'd come home and pay them. It was one of those miraculously symbiotic relationships that kept all three of us above water.

It seems as if all my energies (and certainly most of my income) go into the house. Sometimes I wonder if I shouldn't sell it and move. But I have no idea where I'd go or what I'd do—and God hasn't made anything clear along those lines.

But I get really resentful of all the repairs. It seems that every time I leave for a speaking engagement, the house says "watch this" and something breaks that costs $187 more than I earn.

I complained about this to a friend one afternoon and she said, "Lucy, keeping Hill House going is the best investment you can

make for your girls. You don't have a large
financial estate to leave them and, in this day
and age, it's unlikely they'll ever be able to afford houses of their own. When you die, selling
this house could give them down payments for
their own homes."

I'm not hanging on just for that reason.
And I certainly don't recommend that you do.
You must search your own circumstances.

But, for me, as long as no other path is
clear, I'll stay. I really don't want to start over
in a new community, and I really love this old
house. It is my children's heritage—and my
frustrating delight.

***

For a long time after Louis's death, I felt
enormous guilt about spending money. That
didn't stop me, but I felt guilt.

I am extravagant by nature, but we lived
on such a tight budget that (while Louis was
alive) I never bought something without thinking, "What will Louis say?" Or, "Louis will kill
me for buying this."

Actually, he was pretty good about it.
The fact that I knew he was thrifty kept me
from some ridiculous purchases. But not all the
time.

And he wasn't at all consistent in his

money attitudes. He got furious if I was overdrawn at the bank, but refused to handle the
checkbook.

The first time we were overdrawn after
we were married, he got really angry. I got
angry right back and said, "All right! If you
don't like the way I do it, you do it! Here's the
pen and here's the checkbook!" I didn't pay the
bills. He didn't either. We got an unpleasant
notice enclosed in the electric bill. And I reluctantly picked up the pen again.

Once a month I pulled all the bills off
the clockshelf. Then Louis and I sat down
together at the dining room table and lined out
just how much we could pay on each. And I
wrote the checks.

We had terribly tight times, but they
would have been tighter when he died if I
hadn't been (however reluctantly) the money-
handler in our house.

***

Because of this, I was better equipped to
deal with money matters than many widows.
At least I knew how to write a check. I am ever
amazed at the number of women who don't.
"Oh, my husband handles all the money," say
they smugly, proud of being protected.

Protected! Though they—and their husbands—may not realize it, they are in shackles. Not knowing how to deal with money is as imprisoning as not knowing how to drive a car.

And their situations will be twice as devastating if they are widowed. The national statistics are grim. Over 80% of older Americans who live alone are women. And 85% of surviving spouses are women. On average, women live seven years longer than men, and elderly women outnumber elderly men three-to-two. Just as appalling is the fact that older American women have only 57% of the income of older men.

Now—before you ever have to—is the time to figure out finances.

***

Another aspect of Louis's financial inconsistency always delighted me. We would be broke beyond belief. I'd say something like, "Gee, I wish we could go to the movies." He'd say, "Let's go." I'd say, "Are you crazy? We can't afford it!" And he'd say, "We can't stop living."

One Saturday we went to an auction—a cheap pastime if you only buy ten-cent boxes of junk. I was feeling virtuous that we had a car full of stuff and had only spent $8.00. On the way home, we stopped at an antique shop— just to look. And he bought a mantel clock for

$15.00.

"Are you crazy?" I whispered as I wrote out a sure-to-bounce check. "We can't afford it! And don't you holler at me when we get an overdraft!"

"I think we can get some money up to the bank before it clears," said he, tucking the clock under his arm and heading for the car.

"And besides, we can't stop living."

***

Louis and I never bought a thing we could afford. And we always found some way to pay for it.

But when he died, there was no one to help bear the burden of debt or share the joy of spending. His thumb was off the string of my balloon, as it were, and I did some stupid things.

I still do some stupid things. Like ordering from catalogs. But—in the words of that wise financial seer—*"You can't stop living."*

CHAPTER THIRTEEN
THE QUESTION OF SEX

My increasing dependence on God led me into paeans of gratitude. Every night I got down on my knees by my bed and thanked Him for my work, for my health, for my electric mattress pad. And I thanked Him that I was physically frozen—emotionally iced—and that I had no sexual desires whatsoever. "Just You and me, God, all the way."

That lasted for months. And then the ice broke. Oh, boy. Did it break.

Suddenly, all I wanted was a man's arms around me. All I wanted was loving, tender, glorious affirmation of my womanhood.

All I wanted was sex.

"Why didn't You leave me where I was, God!" I demanded. "What's the point of releasing these desires if You aren't going to send someone along to satisfy them!"

Mind you, I still loved my husband—still grieved for him. But now I had a whole new set of emotional problems to deal with. I flipped right straight back into adolescence. What a bore.

Driving to Chicago, I'd look at truck drivers and wonder, "Is one of these who You have for me?" Or I'd look at men on the street and wonder, "Is one of these the one?"

As I told you, statistics state there is no one for me. A widow who remarries generally does so within a year of her husband's death. The more years pass, the less likely a marriage.

***

Other factors work against remarriage. There are more single women than single men. Men die. Women survive. It makes sense for the future of the race. In a famine, for instance, women who can bear children live much longer than men. But it doesn't make any sense at all for the rest of us single women.

A single man is a social asset because there are so few of them. He receives innumerable invitations—dinners, parties, whatever. Should a man become a widower, the funeral is hardly over before women bearing casseroles arrive on his door step.

A single woman is a social liability because there are so many of us. We hardly ever get a casserole after the funeral.

***

Single women have other problems. Wives fear that we'll poach on their preserves. And wives have considerable justification for this fear. There are lots of married men out there. And some of them are interested in something different. And that something different could be you.

This presents a number of difficulties.

First: If you get involved with a married man, you get morally fogged up. You see affirmation of your own womanhood and to blazes with his wife.

Second: If you get involved with a married man, you get ethically fogged up. You forget that one reason he is so appealing is because some woman—his wife—has helped enhance his potential.

Third: If you get involved with a married

man, you get spiritually fogged up. If you truly depend upon God to guide and support you, you buy a bleak interior life by ignoring His love and choosing the love of someone else's husband.

Fourth: If you get involved with a married man (and you have any awareness at all of how much better your lot is because of the woman's movement), you betray a sister. Ever since Christ set the precedent and hauled Martha out of the kitchen to sit and chat in the living room, generations of women have struggled to help you—right now—through your loss. You have social and political and property rights you would never have had without them. Because of these women—past and present—you are no longer less than a person, simply because you don't have a man. It's just not cricket to cause so much pain to another woman. Think about it. Would you want her to do it to you?

Fifth: If you get involved with a married man, you may lose some of the self-esteem you have fought to recover during the grief process. Dodging around is tacky.

I'm not saying all wives are saints and all husbands are sinners. I'm not saying his wife really doesn't understand him. I'm not saying these relationships can't work out. I'm

not saying you can't live happily ever after. But
I am saying that, if you turn to another woman's husband for release, you may end up with
more problems than you start with.

***

I've gone through a lot of phases during
my sexual awakening. And they weren't easy.
The problem with "going through a phase" is
that I never realize I'm in one until I get out of
it. I always think a particular attitude at a
specific time in my life will last forever. For instance, I was dismayed to think I'd be checking
out truck-drivers until I died. I should have
known that it, too, would pass. And it did.

***

But then I moved into another phase—
one which lasted for years. I never wanted to
marry again.

On the surface, it looked like sour dates
(pun-pardon-please). It looked as if I'd
evaluated the prospects, read the statistics,
determined that no one would marry me anyway, so I'd just live my life as a fascinating, interesting, witty, gracious, charming and basically adorable single.

But it wasn't that at all. I simply
wearied of being a widow. Being a widow is
dull, dismal, and dependent upon a dead hus-

band for status. I decided I'd much rather be a woman. Being a woman is being me.

In the years since Louis's death, I have changed. My ache eased and my pain diminished. I still love Louis. I still miss Louis. But I don't hurt any more. I can look back with joy on Mrs. Louis R. Miele—and rejoice in being Lucy F. Miele.

I've become my own person. I have my own status, and I want people to deal with *me* as *me*. I want them to deal with me because I *live,* not because I *survive.* I don't crave their pity or their concern. I crave their company and their conversation.

But there's more to it than that. For one thing, I remember the Apostle Paul's boast. "I have learned, no matter what state I am in, to be content."

Paul found himself in rotten states. He was in shipwrecks and prisons and hostile mobs and he still insisted he had learned the secret of contentment.

Paul was a lot brighter than I am. I haven't learned it. But it's been given to me— like the peace God gave me not to ask "why?". God gave me contentment.

***

God also gives me a circle of friends who

epitomize the definition of "friend". (A friend is someone who knows all about you and loves you anyway.) He gives me fulfilling—if not full-time—work. He gives me health. He gives me phone calls from my daughters and my father. He gives me visits from my mother-in-law.

He lavishes love upon me.

***

And, selfishly, if popcorn and diet Pepsi in front of the fire sound like a well-balanced, nutritious supper, I don't have to feel guilty about not cooking vegetables for a husband.

If I want to buy a magnetic paper towel holder for the refrigerator door, I don't have to ask permission.

I know these sound like puny pleasures, compared with fireside conversation and snuggling in bed. And so they are. But the important thing is that, over the years, I have ceased that pathetic search for someone to pay the lightbill.

***

There was another (and more personal) reason that I didn't want to marry. Louis knew me. He knew my body in all its stages, from going on yet-another-diet to trying out yet-another-recipe.

He knew my lumps and bumps, as I

knew his. And mine didn't matter to him at all.
One night we were in bed and I was bemoaning
the fact that I'd blown yet-another-diet.

"Darn, I wish I was skinny!"

He reached over and cuddled me into the
curve of his body. "You *are* skinny," he assured
me.

"You're crazy," I said, wiggling my back-
side against him. "I'm not skinny."

"Sure you are," he said, with a cor-
responding wiggle. "Just look at all the skin
you have."

We laughed. And then we loved.

Where, I reasoned, could I find a man
like that? I get tired of holding my stomach in.

So I decided that, if God had marriage in
mind for me, *He* had to do something about it. I
wasn't going on any more blind dates. I wasn't
wasting worry on "is this the one?". I wasn't
holding my stomach in.

"If You want me back cooking vegetables
and defending overdrafts," I told God one
night, "it's up to You."

It really liberated my life.

***

And then one morning—just three
months ago—I got out of bed and started to
dress. Suddenly (as if hit in the stomach) I

doubled over and gasped, "Oh, God! Won't I ever feel a man's arms around me—ever again?"

***

The question of sex?
No answer.

CHAPTER FOURTEEN
THE HORATIO SYNDROME

The same winter Louis died, there came an inundation of books and articles on "out of body" experiences. These detailed case histories of people who (though clinically dead) were brought back to life by extraordinary medical procedures. These people told what death was like. They said there was peace and light and reluctance to come back to life.

Suddenly, it became very fashionable to believe in life after death.

Many dear people (hoping to assuage my grief) sent me materials relating to the experience. I read them, but they didn't impress themselves upon me. I've never had a problem believing in life after death. Even before I awakened spiritually, I'd always felt that there was more reason for existence than to pay my bills and die.

As a matter of fact, the books made me uncomfortable. I had the funny feeling that they verged on being dangerously supernatural.

Now, anybody who believes in God certainly believes in a supernatural Being, right? And that's just fine. But up until several years ago, I had the contemporary rationalist approach to witches and goblins—which is that they are kinda-cute-on-Halloween-but-they-do not-really-exist.

How strange. The Bible states again and again that there are occult powers we cannot comprehend. Even Shakespeare agrees.

"There are more things in heaven and earth, Horatio, than are dreamt of in your philosophy," Hamlet says. I agree. I do believe there are powers in this universe we wot not of. And I further believe that's exactly the way it's supposed to be. We simply shouldn't mess with them.

Ever since I became a Christian—ever since I reluctantly-but-whole-heartedly gave my life to the Lord—I have been made aware of how dangerous it is to look to other powers for guidance.

For instance. I used to read my horoscope. For fun. I didn't *really* believe it, but it was fun to see how wrong it could be.

But sometimes it was right.

And God made it very clear to me that (although these occult powers *can* guide for the moment) He is truly a jealous God. He doesn't want me going anywhere but to Him for guidance. Even in fun.

That's why the Very First Commandment is "Thou shalt love the Lord, thy God, with all thy heart and with all thy soul and with all thy might. This is the *first* and *great* commandment."

Again and again He says, "Thou shalt have no other gods before Me."

He isn't kidding.

Deuteronomy really lays it on the line.

. . .*there shall not be found among you anyone who makes his son or his daughter pass through the fire, one who uses divination, one who practices witchcraft, or one who interprets omens, or a sorcerer. Or one who casts a spell, or a medium, or a spiritist, or one who calls up the dead. For whoever does these things is detestable to the Lord; and because of these detestable things the Lord your God will drive*

*them out before you. You shall be blameless
before the Lord, your God. For those nations,
which you shall dispossess, listen to those who
practice witchcraft and to diviners, but as for
you, the Lord your God has not allowed you to
do so.* (Deut. 18:10-14; NASB).

When did God get really angry at the Is-
raelites? When they started casting gold calves
and looking to them for guidance, that's when.
Every single time they did that, He said, " Take
another lap around Mount Sinai!"

Years ago (for Christmas!), I sent an
ouija board to my brother and his wife. Later, I
became a Christian—and God truly impressed
on my heart my need to trust Him and Him
alone. I started praying against the powers of
*mis*guidance. When (after Louis died) I visited
my brother and sister-in-law in Washington,
DC, I earnestly prayed for the presence of God
—and God alone—in their home.

I don't read my horoscope any more. I
don't even look at it in the paper or magazines.
When people ask me what my "sign" is, I am
constrained to say, "I don't believe that jazz.
I'm a Christian. I guess my sign is the cross."

Unfortunately, I'm a weak vessel. When
they ask me when my birthday is, I do tell
them.

"January third."

And then they nod knowingly and say, "Aha, a Capricorn. I thought so."

What a crock.

Alas, our contemporary society looks for guidance everywhere it can. And (because there *are* occult powers in the universe, Horatio) it can get guidance for the present—for a panacea—for a placebo.

But I believe my God is my true guide.

I am so convinced of this that, though I've met several of the leading sorcerers and diviners of the day at Chicago social affairs, I always flee from them. (Well. Not really. I go to the Ladies' Room.) I'm afraid they'll want to read my palm.

And (though I'm sorely tempted here) I try not to read the strips in Chinese fortune cookies.

Though I have no desire at all to know about the occult, I think it's useful to be aware of it. And I think it's important to know that sometimes a survivor is so lost and so desperate for guidance that he/she turns anywhere.

Going to ouija boards or automatic writing or mediums may give a measure of false comfort—at first. But ultimately, these things turn on you. You become enmeshed in the past instead of getting on with your future.

I know how easy it is to want to keep in touch with the dead. I know the lure of horoscopes and ouija boards. I know how lovely it would be to think that Louis could help me make decisions.

But I also know that God is my only guide. He's forgiven me for all the times I ignorantly sought guidance elsewhere. And He continues to forgive me.

God has also given me real peace about Louis. I don't think Louis's spirit is hanging around. I imagine that, when he got to Heaven, God took him into a screening room and showed him what was going to happen to the girls and me—showed him that he didn't need to worry about us, ever—and then took him off to do His work.

I think Louis is pushing a wheelbarrow around heaven, happily working in the garden.

CHAPTER FIFTEEN
SINGLE FACTS

One of the common facets of recent widowhood (and perhaps of everyone who survives) is to review the funeral, much as if it were a play. We derive a peculiar—but definite—comfort from this. It *matters* if the ushers must set up more chairs. It *matters* if the music is beautiful and meaningful and expressive of the life of the lost. It *matters* if there are flowers.

And we need to talk about it—to discuss it. After all, it is the end of a *life*—not only of the person who died, but of the person who survives. Bear with us. We have no idea what our new life will be. The future is so frightening that we must cling to the life we knew.

***

In order to keep from sobbing at the pain of loss, survivors stretch their mouths in the frozen rictus of a smile. This happens especially in social situations, when the talk turns (as it should, occasionally) to the dead person.

I have two bits of advice regarding this. The first is for the friends of bereaved. Don't be afraid to talk about the loss. It is important for friends to continue to share in the memories. Before Louis died, I thought it would hurt the survivor to talk. I was wrong. No matter how uncomfortable the conversation may be for the friend, it is vital for the survivor. You don't need to talk about it all evening, but (especially if the loss is by death and not divorce) it is healing and loving and right not to let the memories die.

The second bit of advice is for the bereaved. Don't be afraid to talk about the death which affects your life—or the *life* which affected your life.

But don't talk about it all the time.

***

Grief is a full-time job, especially for the

first year. I had no intellectual energy to give to anything else. I had no idea what was going on in the world outside of my loss. People asked me what I thought of the Panama Canal Crisis. Crisis? In Panama? I didn't think anything about it. I couldn't. Louis was dead. That was the overriding, overwhelming crisis in the world.

***

Unless you live alone, you can't imagine how discouraging are the dozens of little shabbies that sprout like dandelions about the place. And you can't imagine how frustrating is the knowledge that you can't summon up the strength or skill to eliminate them. And you can't imagine how good it feels when someone does.

The first year without Louis, it took all my energies to get dressed and give my programs. But various friends showed up at various times to fix light fixtures, change furnace filters, screw in hooks and generally keep the place afloat until I could take the tiller.

What a blessing they were.

***

It is just as important to fix up yourself as to fix up your house. If you look shabby, you feel shabby.

I told you of the friend who took me shopping the very week that Louis died. She knew that if I looked as bad as I felt, I'd feel worse. And she was right.

Putting on your face, getting your hair done, buying a four-dollar frock on sale are all vital ways to combat your own personal shabbies.

***

I kept my wedding ring on my finger for almost a year. Just before Christmas, I was invited to an acquaintance's home for dinner. The other guests were people I've never met, before nor since. But they were used in my grief work.

"Where's your husband?" a man inquired bluntly.

"He's dead," I gasped.

"Then why do you still have your wedding ring on? You're sending the wrong signals. I've been waiting all evening for him to come out of the john."

So I took it off.

It hurt—but I never put it back on my left hand. Instead, I stack three rings on the ring finger of my right hand. First is Louis's wedding ring. Then there's a tiny diamond that belonged to a dear, dead friend of ours. And then there's my wedding ring.

This arrangement accomplishes three things. First—when I look at my hand, I remember two wonderful people in my life. Second—I'm not sending any wrong signals. Third—all that gold is simply stunning.

I'm not saying this will work for you. But consider it. Taking off the ring could break a strand that holds you to your old life—and release you for your new life.

***

Recent singles must *assume* the stance of involvement with others, even if they don't *feel* it. I'm not saying you should become frenetically busy in the beginning. Far from it. Not only is it unwise, it's impossible.

But later on, even if you don't have a real reason to get out of bed (like work or children) do it any way. Take a course, volunteer, do something. You don't need to do it forever—and you won't. But do it. It helps dull the pain, it keeps you involved with living people and (more importantly) it keeps them involved with you until you come to life again.

***

Singles, especially women, find themselves doing things they've never done before. Like hauling hay to mulch the perennial bed. Or filling out financial aid forms. Don't resent having to do them. Accept them as a challenge and you will find satisfaction in being able to accomplish them.

***

I made lots of mistakes that first year after Louis died. I was shy about finding new friends. So I burned out an old friend by making pitiful demands upon his time and presence—a desperate defense against overwhelming loneliness. When you see a friend in full retreat, don't be afraid to back off and say you're sorry. It might not bring back the friend, but it might keep you from making the same mistake twice.

***

As I told you, another loss I suffered was the ability to read. My attention span died. This really concerned me, because reading has ever been my joy. But I couldn't concentrate on anything. I brought home stacks of books from the library, read (maybe) a paragraph in each, and toted them back to the library. One of the signals that life was reassembling itself happened more than a year after Louis's death. I actually finished reading a book.

***

As I moved on into being single (and especially after the girls graduated from high school and left home) I discovered, to my dismay, that I was becoming increasingly self-absorbed.

There is a certain freedom in not having to pack school lunches or make dental appointments or pick children up after play practice. But there is a certain danger in it, as well. Not having anyone else to worry about meant that I had a lot more time to worry about myself.

I tried to counteract this (and I continue in the attempt) by conscious caring for others—especially for other people's children. I show up at choir concerts. I send Valentines. I keep a toy box in the back room.

I think I'm a frustrated grandmother.

***

I have always reveled in exuberant good health. I enjoy feeling well. Therefore, all the articles I read the year after Louis died concerned me. They said that survivors get sick. Stress totally bombards us, and our bodies react with illness.

But during that first year, I wasn't sick at all. I was so grateful and so smug that I was the exception—that God was taking such good care of me.

When that year was over, I fell apart bit-by-bit. I had two major surgeries and (most painful of all) foot surgery. What a bore.

Now I'm now back to exuberant good health. What a blessing.

***

I don't know if singles get sicker than other people, or if our illnesses are exaggerated because we don't have anyone else to worry about. I do know that singles seem to talk more about their health than other people. One reason is that we are on our own. There is no one around to take our temperature. If we don't worry about us, who will?

But hourly bulletins on the state of our sinuses will send friends scurrying away.

***

Singles don't eat very well. At least, I don't. My favorite supper is popcorn and diet Pepsi, which is fast and convenient, but not exactly wholesome nourishment. When I have company for dinner, I'm an enthusiastic, adventurous, wonderful cook. But I don't like scrubbing vegetables and stirring up concoctions and doing dishes, just for me. I simply have no desire to put on a performance if there's no one around to applaud.

So I take vitamins.

***

The bonding of single friends is a family substitute. I don't think couples realize just how close singles become to each other. Within a group of single friends there can be incredible pettiness, jealousy, bickering, support, concern and love. Just like in a family.

***

I once thought the cliché of the old maid and her cats was fiction. But it's fact. I now think every single should have a pet. We need pets for several good reasons.

First: if you live (as I do) in an old house, where things go creak and bump in the night, you can always attribute the strange sounds to the pet. Very comforting.

Second: it's important to have someone else breathing in the house. There is nothing worse than a house with no other presence. (I'm not counting fish. Fish, as far as I'm concerned, don't qualify as pets.)

Third, and most important: it is vital to have someone who's glad to see you when you come home. Daisy Dog (in an excess of ecstasy) does three "welcome" laps around the chicken coop every time I drive up the lane. Pumpkin Cat glares through the door-glass as I fumble for the key, already nagging for his cat chow. Berengeria (my elderly Siamese princess) stalks haughtily from the room on her way upstairs. I'm supposed to follow immediately and get into bed, so she can curl up against me and get warm. As a matter of fact, I'm never supposed to leave that bed.

***

Singles tend to talk about their pets. Too much. It's a curious thing that people who talk endlessly about their children aren't at all interested in your pets—and people who talk endlessly about their pets aren't at all interested in your children. Hmmmm.

***

Unless singles make the effort (and it's a big effort), our social life becomes severely restricted. Single women, especially, need to put away hurts and resentments and throw wonderful parties.

It once bothered me that I give more parties than I go to. I was a social score-keeper and grudge-holder. No longer. I'm just delighted that so many people enjoy coming to my house.

What a gift! What a joy to invite people freely and lovingly—and feel honored when they accept.

***

Time erases bitter memories and underscores good ones. This can be a great comfort to survivors. But we tend (as years go on) to talk about the deceased as if he/she were perfect. Nobody is—or was.

***

But if I'd had three more years to work on Louis, he might have been.

CHAPTER SIXTEEN
FELLOW TRAVELERS

My mother died twenty years ago, and the grief I experienced then was totally different from my grief for Louis. It wasn't as wrenching, as all-encompassing, as long-lasting. My greatest sorrow about my mother is that she died before I matured enough to say, "You know, mother? You were right about. . ."

(I find myself reacting to situations much as she did. Many of the things she taught me which I rejected—simply because she was my mother—I have tried to teach to my children.)

When my mother died, I was a woman grown, with a husband and two children. I was older and more distanced from her and (though I felt her loss keenly) my grief wasn't as terrible as my daughters' grief for Louis. I realized, almost too late, the depth of their sorrow.

A doctor-friend gave me an article which illuminates the feelings children have when a parent dies. According to a survey conducted by psychiatrist Anthony Pietropinto, MD, ("Widows and Widowers"; *Medical Aspects of Human Sexuality;* November, 1985) children, particularly boys, may not openly express their sorrow. "The kids are fine—better than I am," the surviving spouse says. But it is dangerous to underestimate children's grief and turmoil.

The survey showed that a "teenage son is often expected to provide the reassurance and security that the widow formerly received from her husband. . .the youngster may secretly feel imposed upon and unequal to the task."

Additionally, "grown children. . .are often so grief-stricken that they cannot tolerate their parent's intense emotions." Some children also fear that they will be responsible for their parent forever—emotionally and financially.

Although they aren't boys, my daughters

felt much the same way (depended upon; imposed upon; responsible), and I didn't know it. But if you are in a similar situation, I urge you contact your local mental health facility. There are peer groups and counseling and grief therapy for young people. If I had known about them when we needed them, I'd have used them.

***

Men have no easier time coping with the death of a spouse than women do. As a matter of fact (according to the same survey) a significant majority of physicians feel that men have a more difficult time. Dr. Pietropinto points out several reasons:

For one thing, men can't cry. They have no outlet for their grief. Society expects women to cry, but men must be stoical. And because they suffer in silence, they suffer more.

A woman's friends and relatives are more adept at providing emotional support than a man's. Women will hug and comfort. But a widower's male friends simply are not e- quipped to deal with open displays of emotion. And men need hugging and comforting, too.

Commonly, men lose a lot of weight. First of all, many men simply don't understand such basic activities of daily life as marketing and cooking. Secondly, their depression makes it even more difficult to expend effort on a new

task like meal preparation.
*Men are more apt to turn to alcohol than women. This could lead to malnutrition and aggravate other health problems.

Alcohol abuse can lead to emotional problems, as well. Since alcohol is a depressant, not a stimulant, it can deepen the survivor's natural depression after loss. It can also prolong the grief process by suspending the user in alcoholic limbo.

(Dependency on tranquilizers is common among women. Though I yearned for oblivion, I refused to take even a sleeping pill. I knew that the grief and loss would still be there when I woke up.)

The universal male reluctance to seek medical care also works against a man. It is viewed as acquiescence to weakness and (without his wife to nag him into a doctor's appointment) he ignores his body's warnings.

It's no wonder that more men than women die shortly after the loss of a spouse.

If you are a grieving man, this information shouldn't frighten you. It should help you. If you have a map of unknown country, it helps you get through it. You need to cry and cook and go to the doctor and find a listener and pray.

If you are a friend of a grieving man, you

need to hug and comfort and encourage and listen and pray.

***

Another grief impossible to understand unless you have experienced it is the grief of parents for a dead child. The loss of a child may be the most devastating experience a parent can endure. Not only is there immediate loss—there are all the milestones down through the future where the loss will be felt. Graduation. Marriage. Grandchildren.

You have the Guilties and the Angries and the Lonelies. And your Lonelies seem to last forever. Because there are other people's children. All around you. Every time you see a child, your pain returns.

Support groups—people banding together who have experienced the same type of loss—can bring release and help. *Compassionate Friends* is the name of one such group. Their national office is:

Compassionate Friends, Inc.
PO Box 3696
Oak Brook, IL 60522
312-990-0010

Parent Bereavement Outreach (535 16th St., Santa Monica, CA 90402) serves the greater Los Angeles area. One of its leaders,

Lee Schmidt, R.N., M.N., has compiled a list of loving behavior for helping bereaved parents.

Though worded specifically for comforting parents who have lost children, the suggestions are universally applicable.

DO. . .

. . .let your genuine concern and caring show.

. . .be available to listen, to run errands, to help with the other children, or whatever else seems needed at the time.

. . .say you are sorry about what happened to their child and for their pain.

. . .allow them to express as much grief as they are feeling at the moment and are willing to share.

. . .encourage them to be patient with themselves, not to expect too much of themselves and not to impose any "shoulds" on themselves.

. . .allow them to talk about the child they have lost as much and as often as they want to.

. . .talk about the special, endearing qualities of the child they've lost.

. . .give special attention to their other children—at the funeral and in the months to come. They, too, are hurt and confused and in need of attention which their parents may not be able to give at this time.

. . .reassure them that they did everything they could, that the medical care their child received was the best, or whatever else you know to be true and positive about the care given to their child.

DON'T. . .

. . .say you know how they feel, unless you've lost a child yourself.

. . . say "you ought to be feeling better by now" or anything else that implies a judgment about their feelings.

. . .tell them what they should feel or do.

. . .change the subject when they mention the dead child.

. . .avoid mentioning the child's name out of fear of reminding them of their pain.

. . .try to find something positive (e.g., a moral lesson, closer family ties, how they can help others with similar loss) about the child's death.

. . .point out that at least they have their other children. Children are not interchangeable. They cannot replace each other.

. . . say that they can always have another child. Even if they want to and could, another child would not replace the child they have lost.

. . .suggest that they should be grateful for their other children. Grief over the loss of one child does not discount parents' love and appreciation of their living children.

. . .make any comments which in any way suggest that the care given their dead child at home, in the emergency room, hospital or wherever was inadequate.

. . .avoid them because you are uncomfortable. Being avoided by friends adds pain to an already intolerably painful experience.

AND ABOVE ALL. . .

. . .don't let your own sense of helplessness keep you from reaching out to bereaved parents.

(*Do's and Don'ts for Helping Bereaved Parents*, © 1979 Lee Schmidt)

***

But there is yet another group that grieves—a group that is often overlooked. Divorcées.

I have spoken frequently to groups about my experiences as a widow and, without exception, women with tears in their eyes come to me and say, "Lucy—we have the very same

thing. We have the Guilties and the Angries
and the Crazies and the Poverties and the
Lonelies. But it's worse with us. We have 'walking around dead'. That man is still alive.''

So often these are wives whose husbands
have left them for younger women. Not only do
they suffer through all the stages of grief—they
also have the teeth of rejection gnawing at
their very souls.

Many of these divorcées also have an
imaginary scenario, wherein the ex-husband
will tire of his girlfriend and return to the com-
forts of home-cooking. One woman I know persisted in this fantasy for years, even though
her ex-husband remarried and had three
children. She finally shook loose, moved to
Florida, got a job as social director of a country
club, met a man, married, and is (according to
her last Christmas letter) unbelievably happy
and fulfilled.

(Divorcées are more likely to remarry
than widows, for the simple reason that the
average widow is in her sixties and the average
divorced woman is in her thirties or forties. My
friend, however, beat the statistics. She was
over fifty when she remarried.)

The divorced women who talk with me
say that, though their marriages are dissolved,
there are still painful strands which bind them

to their ex-husbands. Many of them have
young or adolescent children to support and
(all too frequently) must continually seek child-
support from their ex-husbands.

They seem almost envious of my status
as a widow.

***

I simply can't begin to address the survivors of people who have committed suicide. I
know that you go through all the stages—but
longer, harder, deeper. And I think that the
most long-term, most harmful stage you experience is the Guilties.

Taking one's life is perhaps the most
personal, most lonely act in existence. No one
else is responsible for it. But you, the survivor,
are responsible if you let your own life be lost
in guilt. Again, it takes a conscious, continuing
effort of will to box up those Guilties and shove
them back on the closet shelf.

Do reach out. Do seek counsel. I urge
you to contact your local mental health facility.

And prayer helps, too.

***

No one has the corner on heartache.
Husbands, wives, children, parents, mothers,
fathers, brothers, sisters—everyone will lose
someone. It is part of the human condition.

I pray that my experiences help you cope with loss. I never consciously planned to cope—I just muddled through. But I know I would never have muddled through the past eight years with as much joy if it hadn't been for two great gifts—my faith and my friends.

My faith in Jesus Christ has been the solid rock in a universe that blew apart when my husband died. My awareness that I don't *have* to do it all myself—that I have a loving, caring Creator who is constantly there, eager to help—means sanity for me. I can't depend on my husband. I certainly can't depend on me. I have to depend on Him.

Friends are my other great gift. They laugh and cry and party and pray with me.

Thank God.

CHAPTER SEVENTEEN
GOD IS GREAT, GOD IS GOOD

The main message I have for you is that, someday, you may find yourself with the Guilties, the Angries, the Crazies, the Poverties and the Lonelies. You can get through them—if you trust God.

Looking back, I can see how great and good He is.

God gave me work, to support my family.

God gave me friends, whom He impels to do loving, lovely things.

God gave me assurance that Louis is, indeed, with Him.

God gave me a loving memory of the last time I saw Louis. Our last words could have been unloving.

We only had one car and, if I needed it during the day, I had to drive him to work. Sometimes I didn't get him up to school as early as he thought I should. Sometimes he was only five minutes early, instead of ten. Sometimes I snapped out "good*bye*" and sometimes he slammed the car door and sometimes I spun the wheels on the parking lot gravel. Our last time together could have been like that, and he could have gone into the school building and died.

But it wasn't. Instead it was filled with assurance of mutual love.

God gave me circumstances that allowed Louis to have the car that day. He drove to town. He didn't die alone.

The girls and I could have walked in late that night and found him dead, on the sofa in the library. We didn't.

God gave us two, whole, beautiful snow days before Louis died. They were times of sharing and quiet appreciation—times of contentment and love.

And once upon a time—long, long ago— God looked down and said, "I'm going to do something super for Lucy."

And He gave me Louis.

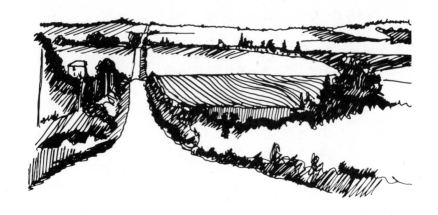

LUCY'S SONG

He saw the world through very gentle eyes,
He saw the person, never the disguise,
And every day was summer.

Now let him find the gold in fields of growing grain,
And let him touch the cloud that sends the silver
rain,
And wrap him in a rainbow.

And now he waits where Time has never been,
Where silent songs become the whispering wind,
And still, his love surrounds me.

Now let him fly where stars of diamond are made,
And let him run through fields of emerald and jade,
And shelter him with moonbeams.

And tell him that I love him.

Patricia Benton Johnson